# speak
# POWER,
# speak
# WEALTH,
# and speak
# FREEDOM

## Paradigm Processing — Tearing Down the Walls

### DR. WILLIAM A. MARTIN

10 09 08   6 5 4 3 2 1
First Edition

Edited by Dr. William A. Martin and Diane Martin
Printed by United Graphics Inc.
Cover and interior book layout design by Borel Graphics
Cover illustration by Kamaga

United States ISBN Agency
ISBN 13: 978-0-9802176-9-8

Disclaimer:
The following stories are true. Names have been changed or eliminated for confidential reasons. They depict personal experiences, successes, and failures. Some of the names have been changed or excluded to protect those individuals who did not want to be named. Any similarities to events are completely coincidental.

# Acknowledgements

There are many, many people – all of them have been responsible for the completion of this paradigm. However, first, I want to acknowledge my personal divine spirit, and those who played a pivotal part in my life's journey and the development of my spiritual beliefs. I would also like to extend a very zealous thank you to the members of my immediate family who knowingly or unknowingly led to the completion and ideology of this book. A special thanks to my wife, Diane, without her motivation and encouragement I would not have completed it.

# Contents

# Contents

"Courage is not the absence of fear;
it is the presence of fear and the
courage to continue on anyway."

**- Mark Twain**

# Preface

$S$ peak Power, Speak Wealth and Speak Freedom Paradigm Processing: Tearing down the walls is a multidisciplinary book. It "tears down the walls" between adult education, motivational advising, counseling, and mentoring; between higher education and learning from experience, between for-profit business and philanthropy, between your physical mind and your conscious spiritual self. It "tears down the walls" between being a self-centered leader, and being a leader with courage and conviction. It is that space between, before, and around a Paradigm Shift to holistic wealth and health. Paradigm Processing is a feeling of fondness before action, feelings of affection after deeds, and finally a deep sense of love and understanding over-time.

The goal of this book is to teach its readers how they can use their mental senses to create a paradigm where needed to better their lives and the lives of those around them. The philosophy is that many human beings do not use their spirit, faith, sense of worth, emotions, and feelings to control their circumstances. They do not take the time to map their future from their visions of who they should and want to be over time. I'm a true believer that there is a "time" and a place for everything and when life found it befitting it created an atmosphere where time and space came together, an important element of Paradigm Processing. In other words, my life experiences were Paradigm Processing experiences that led to a Paradigm Shift, which is when the book was actually written, published, and distributed. I can confidently say that the only thing between you and wealth is time, which is relative to your experiences. You can "Speak Power, Speak Wealth, and Speak Freedom" into the physical with unyielding faith.

You are reading this book "in the now", and as you continue to read, you will begin to see yourself in a future of wealth, health, joy, faith, and righteousness – those unforeseen changes that happen throughout life actually occurring in the present; even with those unforeseen humanistic changes that occur throughout life.

This book is designed to supply you with a method that is guaranteed to make your vision, goals, and dreams come true. This book focuses on the viewpoints of relationships and positive motivational discourse. The exclusive advantage of this book lies in the behavioral science disciplines, which are incorporated in the ideology. It includes the manner in which we develop our paradigm. The variety of information for inclusion has been made with a single objective: to describe and depict the major components and elements of Paradigm Processing that will make you holistically wealthy. This book helps you to build and maintain a mental map from a humanistic approach to becoming holistically wealthy in faith, in health, in finances, in the spirit, and through the physical, sociological, and psychological sphere.

This book will give you an undeniable interpretation of the significance of real world wealth. That wealth that is associated with thinking, and acting. It is the sphere and the holistic approach to believing that true faith, hard and smart work would equal success squared. It is my vision that all levels of your life would be full of joy and happiness. I hope that the information included is not limited, but motivated by the elements of the human characteristics and associations of the mind, the body and the spirit. Most importantly, it is for the general reader whose exclusive purpose is to feel better about him or her by living and growing in a spirit of joy.

It starts with Paradigm Processing your mind, your worldview, and your emotional panoramic view displayed to individuals every moment of the day. The feelings and emotions we have as human beings that are displayed through all forms of discourse; in writings, discussions, and body language that another person can view in their paradigm implicitly and explicitly throughout their life. Whether an individual is using visual aids, written language, or any form of discourse that can be connected to human consumption politically, socially, educationally or economically, it all has an effect on paradigms. The written language in this book allowed me to use examples to help the reader to announce and examine goals – not generic goals – real life-long goals that will guarantee wealth and happiness for generations.

I guarantee that after reading this book, there will be a change in your panoramic view of the world, and in a large part, a form of human growth that will make you more receptive to new experiences. Individual experiences that will lead to great things, but most importantly, great wealth because now we are "tearing down the walls" that have hindered you from success in the past.

# Chapter 1

## *Theoretical Framework: The 4Rs and the Paradigm Processing Model*

Despite what many school texts would lead us to believe, becoming wealthy is not a closed art. I have spent almost my entire mentoring, coaching, motivating, advising, and counseling career proving to people that it is easy to have anything that they desire, provided they follow a few simple, but important rules:

- **Reflection,**
- **Reciprocal Learning,**
- **Research/Resources, and**
- **Responsibility to the community (4R Model)**

The acronym 4R includes Reflection, Reciprocal Learning, Research/Resource, and Responsibility to the community. The 4R Model is a problem solving formula that works with anyone and any type of instruction and/or situation. This model is built on the framework of education and business, but can easily be applied to your life. However, it is designed to encompass the culture, competency, and the relationship of theoretical content and practice. The 4R Model is the beginning point that connects individuals to their external and internal world; reflect on your experiences, on what coaches, mentors, and lecturers are trying to impart (reciprocal learning), learn from one another, other students, coaches, mentors, and advisors, research those questions that could not be answered during reciprocal learning, and finally responsi-bility to the community, to yourself, and to your fellow man/woman.

When I became an advisor and lecturer, I did not know the importance of reflection. As a lecturer, I taught my first classes pretty much like a machine. However, I soon discovered that I was on the wrong track. I was trying to teach and advise adults in areas that did not meet their holistic needs. I was trying to teach adults as though they were one entity and not a singular personality. What the adult student wanted was enough courage to stand-up and make a clear, coherent decision about what would bring him or her joy, and happiness in their quest to obtain a higher education and a better understanding of their life goals.

It was not long before I threw the old rigid textbooks out of the window, got right up there on the podium in the classroom and began a revised approach to old ideas by introducing a few simple new ideas. I began to work with students individually by incorporating the 4R Model, starting with an icebreaker. The icebreaker encouraged students to do a self-assessment of their true needs. It worked, because they kept coming back for more coaching and mentoring in an attempt to discover new options to help them achieve their goals.

During the icebreaker, the students and I always found someone in the class who had the same vision, or someone who could help him or her with their vision. They really wanted to be happy with their work, wealthy enough to take care of their families, healthy, and stress free. Most of them felt a need to change their lives for the better, but the lack of faith and self-confidence to go for their visions created a wall that they were afraid to climb. After speaking with fellow classmates, they were able to see the possibilities. They were excited and anxious to learn. They were so grateful for having a coach, and a course that allowed them to achieve something so rewarding – a piece to the puzzle that completed their journey toward a life full of joy.

I have mentored hundreds of people, but one mentee comes to mind because of the dramatic impact their story had on me. Some years ago, shortly after I joined the Continuing Education and Nontraditional Degree Programs at Chicago State University (CSU), I met a young man who was thinking about changing his major from nursing to one of our nontraditional majors. He walked into my office and said, "I majored in nursing, but I am not happy with my decision." I told him that he was too young to enter one of our Nontraditional Degree Programs because of the program's requirements. To understand what exactly he was trying to accomplish, I went on to talk to him about what would bring him joy in life, and what was it that he did continually in good or bad times. He said, "I love history." He stated, "You can always find me watching the History channel or reading a history book." I watched his mannerisms and how he smiled throughout the conversation. I decided to become his mentor and advised that young man to change his major to what would make him happy. He changed his major from nursing to history. Throughout his academic journey, he visited me often to provide updates about his grades and needs (if any). Each visit, we discussed how much he was enjoying his classes, how he enjoyed the curriculum, and how excited he was about applying the information learned to other aspects of his life. He told me often how the information he had received from his classes helped him to have a better sense of himself. He graduated with his undergraduate degree in history from CSU in one year. Later, he received a fellowship from one of the largest universities in Illinois to work on his Master's degree in History.

As his mentor, I assured him, on the basis of my experiences with men and women in similar positions, that he would succeed. He was so happy to complete his undergraduate degree and then being accepted into a topnotch program at another university that a couple of months later he called me wanting information on how to earn his doctorate free of cost. In our conversation, I asked him whether my prediction that he would grow wealthy and healthy once he set on a mission to take care of his hopes and dreams had come true, he laughed, and stated, "Absolutely."

In order for these things to happen in your life, you must first confess that your life is missing something and that you want to make a change. Then seek out individuals who can help guide you in your quest - a coach or mentor can help you to find what you are looking for. To say that there is a need for a change is not an admission that something is broken; it just means that something is missing and you may need help figuring out what that is.

As a coach and mentor, the pleasure I get in giving makes me healthy and socially wealthy. The services I can deliver in the community are among the most gratifying things in my life. I feel that I owe it to people to share the things that I have learned because so many mentors and coaches in my community have done the same for me. I and many other people coach and mentor with the hope that their story will inspire people.

I have seen hundreds of similar miracles happen in my courses and in my life. I have seen men and women whose lives were transformed by helping them to connect with other people (i.e., coaches and mentors) with similar visions and goals. Many of the people who have connected with others in their field had received promotions far beyond their dreams. Others had obtained positions of prominence in their businesses, professions, and communities because they confessed and conquered their fear by stepping out of the cocoon they called their lives. Sometimes this has been done by means of a single speech delivered at the right moment, by the right person. I can remember a sermon given by a visiting speaker at my church. The speaker changed my life by reinforcing my belief in speaking everything you want into existence.

I remember that on that day, I did not want to go to church because I was writing my book. I had so much work to do with the courses that I was teaching and the reports I needed to complete for the university. Generally, when I feel (and the key word is "feel") something so deeply, there is something special in store for me that day, and it was. The preacher's first words were, "Talk your way into Heaven." He went on to say, "Speak and praise aloud, take control of your life with your words and all of your blessings will gravitate to you." Then he said, "Get out of your seat, get rid of your fears of praising in public because nobody is looking at you, and remember that it is not about you, it is about getting closer to Heaven through praise." He spoke of a form of praise that flows from your lips with enthusiasm, fearlessness, and joy. In fact, he stated, "Confessing your fears is the first step to speaking and receiving your blessings." Sounds like a miracle, doesn't it? It is an everyday miracle of conquering fears by confessing fear, and asking for help and believing that there is a higher power that is going to help you to overcome it.

Reflect and think of people who have come into your life who believed in you and your vision, and stated, "Call me, I can help." These people might be relatives or friends of the family, a teacher, a clergy-man, or anybody who wanted to step in and help. They asked to help you refine, define, and achieve your vision. Now look around you. There are people all around you willing to help you achieve your goals - reach your dreams. This could be people sitting right next to you right now. So what's the first step? Start a conversation. Speak openly and honestly about your needs and wait faithfully for the help.

Now, make a list of five potential mentors who can help you to see and achieve your vision.

_____

_____

_____

_____

_____

Make definite and specific plans for contacting these potential mentors and for seeking their guidance. It is up to you to contact these individuals, to have enough faith in their guidance that it will eradicate any fear that you may have had.

As you reflect on the successes and failures of your past, you begin to see how powerful you are, how you have spoken things into existence through prayer (e.g., discourse with yourself) or how discourse with and through others has had a profound effect on your life. I am talking about a power that will make people sit up and take notice. They will see the joy of life in your actions, even if your actions failed the first ten times, it doesn't matter. It is both, the successes and failures, that have shaped you into the incredible person you have become.

In short, in terms of the 4R Model, reserve power is the ability to reflect on experiences that would boost your confidence at any given time. The millionaires that have sat in my office have all said one thing about their experiences and that is they failed many times before they were successful, but they never gave up. The failures provided them with the reserve power to continue to look for the gifts presented to them through looking within themselves for the strength to go on and through discourse with others.

I have stepped out on faith many times throughout my life. I think we all try many things throughout life, because we are inquisitive by nature. However, I also believe that most of us do not have true faith in our ability to be successful. I think we believe that we are the most gifted in countless areas, until we do it with people that are highly proficient in those areas. For example, I was watching the Gospel Awards on television, and a church choir sang a song that brought tears to my eyes. They had a female lead singer that was very talented. However, right after that choir sang, Ms. Yolanda Adams came to the stage and displayed why she has won so many awards.

Her gifts were far more superior to the lead singer of that choir. There were no comparisons; her voice was a well-trained instrument. At that time, place, and space I could feel her joy, I could see that she was very gifted, and had chosen a song that intensified her vision, her faith, and a spirit of victory. Singing is the form of discourse Ms. Adams and other gospel singers use to project their spirit, faith, future of joy and victory. I believe that is why so many of us are drawn to their music. It is intoxicating and evokes emotions that we are not willing to expose on a daily basis. The music and the lyrics allows us to experience our pain, if only in our minds, and allows us to find hope in the midst of it.

On another occasion, a real estate millionaire walked into my office to find out about the university's nontraditional degree programs. We talked for an hour and a half. We talked about the programs the university had to offer and how she could accomplish her goals of graduating from one of the best public universities in the state. She told me how she made several million dollars in real estate and lost it all. Nevertheless, she also stated, "It's not a big deal. I'll make it again." I was in shock. It didn't bother her that she lost it all. Her declaration to regain her wealth, as if it was something as simple as finding her car in a crowded parking lot, intrigued me. We continued to talk and through our discourse, I found that the option to be wealthy was as simple as proclaiming it, getting up, and making it happen.

Just like many of the millionaires that have come into my office, and I have read about, her future in wealth bore-fruit from her discourse and actions. She was very confident in her ability to grow wealthy, and she was not afraid to say it. Currently she has seven million dollars in the bank and 110 properties all over the country. Now, I have real estate investments, but she was clearly better at it than I was at that time and place. I asked how she did it – how did she become a real estate millionaire? She stated that, "You must try to get ten times as much information, sometimes a hundred times as much education about what would bring you joy. I can teach you in ten minutes how to go out and acquire property. However, I could never tell you what will bring you joy or success." In other words, it takes time and work to get to anything that you are passionate about doing in life, but the joy is magnified ten times over when it is accomplished. She also stated that she believed that once you find that one thing that you are passionate about, "Your will, will be true to your vision and your gift, and the victory will be yours even in times of problems because you have developed the ability to learn from your experiences."

You, too, can acquire reserve power by finding that one thing that brings you joy and holding on to that joy with true faith. Do not put it off another day, it is your time, write it down and post it on your wall to get you ready to do what you have to do to obtain the wealth and health that is rightfully yours. Time you ordinarily spend daydreaming, while you are driving home, waiting for a bus, or riding the subway, can be devoted to mulling over the next thing you need to do to obtain that joy. It is during this incubation period that flashes of insight will come and your conscious and subconscious mind will work through it giving you the answers you seek.

Reflection:

What is my gift?

_____

_____

_____

_____

_____

Why do I believe in this gift?

_____

_____

_____

_____

When did I ever see this gift exemplified in real life?

_____

_____

_____

_____

_____

How, precisely, am I going to use this gift?

_____

_____

_____

_____

_____

**(Read Aloud)**
**I will take account of my vision.**

In order to take account of your vision, you must ask yourself several questions. What is it that you enjoy doing most? What gives your life meaning? What were you called to do? What is your purpose? What do you look forward to doing more than anything else?

_____

_____

_____

_____

_____

It is far easier to go into something just for the money, or skim over the surface of your visions than to dig down deep for the faith to create joy and wealth in your life. When you take the easy way out, you make little or no attempt for happiness. After you have narrowed your vision down to what would bring meaning to your life and what would make you happy, have discourse with yourself with the same conviction and enthusiasm as when you are talking to others. The next step is to ask yourself several more questions that will deepen your understanding of your vision, and help you to take account of your vision with the gifts or talents that you were born with, and called to do by the spirit. Prepare yourself to go for your goals using those gifts and talents.

**(Read Aloud)**
**I will live in the present, reflect on the past, and believe that my future is filled with wealth and joy.**

The 4R Paradigm Processing Model is a structured coaching methodology. It is about Paradigm Processing through discourse within a group setting. It is based on a socialization process. Socialization, according to Merriam Webster (1977), "is the process by which a human being beginning at infancy acquires the habits, beliefs, and accumulated knowledge of society through education and training for adult status." Socialization enhances the level of perception of norms and values, which are the ground-rules of the 4R Model. I focus on the 4R Model throughout the book in many forms. The model was developed with any type of situation in mind. The 4R Model includes your spirit, faith, and the need to live victorious. The goals of the model are to create a society of spiritual and faithful people living victorious with discourse. In that discourse, we reflect on the subject, the idea, and the philosophy at hand.

In the second "R", we engage in reciprocal learning by introducing ourselves to someone with knowledge of the subject – coming together and exchanging ideas. There's always a forum in which this can occur; a church, grocery store, PTA meeting, anywhere. By expressing your desires, you put them into the universe thereby causing a "boomerang effect" drawing that same energy or people that exude that type of energy back to you. So, on the flip side of that, you have to be careful about the type of discourse you have with others. If you talk negative about yourself and the things that you want to achieve then "negative" things will come back or happen to you – speak success or positive about yourself and your goals and positive things will happen in your life. Often, I have heard, "When praises go up, blessings come down" and wondered to myself, "How does this work?" I mean, analytically, I look up, "praise", and because of it, I will be blessed. How does that work? Well, without stating the obvious, the concept works on the premise that we must speak the things that we want into existence – believe that what we want will come to us and begin to live our lives as if what we have asked for already exists in the physical. For example, if we lift our heads and ask that we no longer have to suffer from a "lack of", we begin to praise because we know that by asking with true faith, that things will be okay. Now, we can proceed with our lives without worrying about not having what we need to survive.

**(Read Aloud)**
**I will draw people to me with charismatic joy.**

The action-reaction in the model affects our ability and need to get what we want out of life. It affects our willingness to give back to the community, the positive characteristics in us all, and the charismatic discourse with others. I am talking about a charisma that magnetizes people to our goals, visions, outcomes, and perceptions. The model is excellent for any stage of life that you are in (i.e., elderly, young, or middle age). Theorists such as Erickson have suggested that, "Major aspects of human development unfold in a series of life stages." (Erickson, 1952, also, cited in Ormrod, 1995) Paradigm Processing is "a method of changing social and individual line-of-sight with theory."

The Paradigm Processing agenda and ideology is utilitarian, in that it relates to diverse differences from the dominant philosophy of faith, education, from culture to subcultures, and in any social environment. According to Kuhn (1962), the inventor of the term and ideology "paradigm" thought it to be only about scientific authenticity, but Kuhn later made connections between paradigms and sociological value, which is the foundation of this theoretical framework, identity socialization from "Paradigm Processing" (Barnes, 1982). Kuhn discovered that there are many foundations and dimensions to paradigms, but for the purpose of this portion of the analysis, we will look at the linkages as a Paradigm Processing function. In other words, Paradigm Processing is one of the associations to social linkage, and Paradigm Shifts.

The third "R", research, begins after there is no resolution to unsolved issues. A perfect example of research comes from a moment shared with my son. He has a tendency to, instead of looking up things in the dictionary himself, he comes to me and expects me to give him all of the answers. I usually reply to his requests by saying, "Look it up yourself." He hates this because he wants me to make it easy for him – just give him the answers. I've told him, on many occasions that the best way to hide something from someone is to put it in a book. I know this comment may sound negative, but we often miss out on great things because we don't want to put in the work or make an effort to find the answers ourselves. As a result of my constant insistence that he finds or researches the answers himself, I often find him in the library or reading a book; he is smarter because of it.

At the completion of the research, it is the responsibility (the fourth "R") of the researchers to report the findings to others for the betterment of human kind. For the model to work completely, you have to give back to your community and society. This concept is considered as "passing the torch." Now that you have found the answers that many are looking for, you have a responsibility to pass the information on to others. What they do with the information is not of your concern. You have done what is required of you. If they don't do anything with the information that you've given them then it's on them. "You can lead a horse to water, but you can't make them drink." In other words, "You can show people the way to do things, but you can't force them to act," (The New Dictionary of Cultural Literacy, 2002)

**(Read Aloud)**
**Reflection is the process of deep consideration of past and present events.**

Now that we've briefly reviewed the four "Rs", let's revisit the first "R" which is called Reflection. Reflection is introduced and becomes an on-going process; Paradigm Processing within the environment, personal relationships, culture, and most importantly ideology. In this case, the perception we have about our ability to become holistically wealthy, our ability to magnetize positive relationships, and the ability to give back to society. Mezirow and Brookfield, (cited in Cranton, 1994) states, "Critical reflection is almost always stimulated by the environment and discussion with others." Individuals reflect on their own learning from discourse and research, including that additional knowledge they hope to gain and how that knowledge can be used in the context of their faith, their paradigm, their education, wealth, health, etc.

Eraut (2002) found that, reflection is triggered by the recognition that in some respects the situation is not normal and therefore is in need of special attention. The trigger may be an unexpected action or outcome, explicit or implicit, positive or negative, or just an intuitive feeling that something is not quite right. Thus, what may have begun as a routine situation grew to be perceived as problematic or potentially problematic in nature. For example, as a person in expectation of wealth and victory, I reflect on the area that would magnetize wealth to me. What becomes problematic is the responsibility that comes along with it. Questions will arise. Should I give it all away? Should I save it for a rainy day? Should I invest it? Then there's the issue that arises when family and friends find out that you've obtained wealth. The weight could become potentially heavy for the weak, that is where the importance of faith steps in and gives us the strength and the answers to handle the situation.

**(Read Aloud)**
**In a mirror, the image looking back at me is considered a reflection. "Do I like what I see?"**

This also pertains to reflection. Actually, this is where everything begins. There is a term called, Sankofa. Sankofa states that, "To know where you are going, you must first know where you've been." This is when we take inventory of ourselves. We have to take account of our accomplishments and decide if we are happy with what we've done. Now many of us may find this process difficult because it requires a certain level of honesty. Some of us, outside of getting out of bed every day, can't really say that they've done much with their lives and that's tragic. These people we will refer to as the "living dead." These are people who are physically alive. They have a pulse, but are not living. They live their lives everyday doing nothing, accomplishing nothing, by assuming the lives of others, and by living vicariously through them. What will their legacy be? These people leave nothing behind because they've done nothing. Reflection gives us the opportunity to prevent these inadequacies from happening. Make a list of what you've done and what you would like to do. The things you've done will become your legacy while the things you would like to do will now become your life goals. We will call it our "to do" list.

Practice: Create a list of all of the things that you have done.

_____

_____

_____

_____

_____

_____

_____

Practice: Now create your "to do" list.

_____

_____

_____

_____

_____

_____

_____

_____

_____

_____

_____

## Reflection

Reflection can occur psychologically, sociologically, and through the physical environment via colors, signs, and artifacts. One of the things I appreciate about my life is my past. The past physical environments my family and I were in and the psychological effect it had on me.

For me, my past was a result of creative tension. Webster (1986) defines tension "as two balancing forces causing or tending to cause extension." Tension can also be psychologically expressive caused by an uneasy force. For example, if you look at my life as though it was a rubberband, my life experiences had two forces at work, one pulling in one direction and the other pulling in the opposite direction. Over-time, the rubberband will either break or seek resolution. If the rubberband seeks resolution, it would relax, creating a momentum to propel forward. Aim the rubberband at a specific destination, and it will have a focused forward momentum. In other words, use reflections too consciously propel yourself forward into your victorious future.

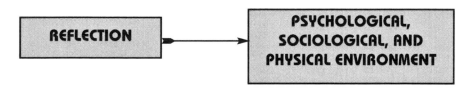

**FIGURE 1.** *Reflection*

## Reciprocal Learning

The second "R" refers to Reciprocal Learning. Following and/or during reflection; Reciprocal Learning takes place within discourse, past victories, failures, and their economic, social, and cultural context. The knowledge gained is either self-selectively proscribed by some form of discourse, through research and faith, or through others' reflections.

To ensure a meaningful learning experience for all, facilitation of the discourse must have been weighed prior to "Reflection and Reciprocal

Learning." In other words, when you have discourse, have your goal and vision in mind. It is the role of the individual to guide the use of "socio-cultural" discourse as the basis of this model according to Raiskums (2001). The Socio-cultural Frame is "a perspective of adult development involving both social and cultural factors" (Caffarella, 2000: personal communication, November 13, 2000). For example, if you have discourse with someone who knows something about a certain topic, you will come to know what he or she knows. Likewise, if you have discourse with someone who does not know anything you will both suffer and more importantly, hinder the growth of everyone you share that information with.

He or she will not learn from you and you will not learn from him or her if the discourse is not all-embracing. Remember, if there is no education, experiential learning, or wisdom to base your philosophy on then no one will embrace your goals and visions. There has not been a class that I have taught where I did not learn something important from one of my students. In this model, the learning becomes more than a psychological conflux of knowledge, learner, and facilitator's work. The model is built on the continually changing facts, and research within the socio-cultural environment.

Merriam & Cafferella (1999) suggested that socio-cultural learning is defined as an act that transforms roles and identity; an identity or paradigm transformation that occurs when people join social groups after participating in discourse regardless of the discussion. It is Paradigm Processing from the experienced members, but it is also influenced by knowledge of the subject or perception of some experience. Pratt & Nesbit (2000) concurred stating that the construction of a group of community learners may be keys to an individual learner's success. In other words, community knowledge is most likely transmitted best in a group, and where Reciprocal Learning takes place. Additionally, Paradigm Processing is in union with reflection, which can also occur from the perceptions and experiences in the physical, psychological, and sociological environment without a total Paradigm Shift (See Figure 2).

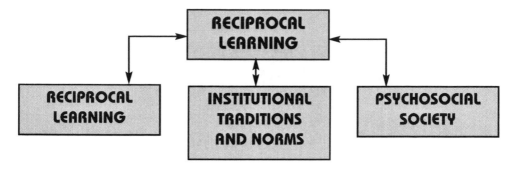

**FIGURE 2.** *Reciprocal Learning*

What does it mean to really talk to someone? What does it mean to have a truly reciprocal learning experience with someone? What does it mean to really listen to someone? Hearing and listening is not the same thing, although they are interconnected. On a basic level, it is that physical interconnected transmission and unwilling transmission of knowledge. That is the non-verbal communication and information that is unconsciously and consciously shared between individuals during human connections. Not to oversimplify, however, we might say that hearing is a physiological progression whereas listening is a psychological development. The physiological progression is the sound waves entering the outer ear and transmitted to the eardrum, converted into mechanical vibrations in the middle ear, and changed in the inner ear in electrical impulses that travel to the brain (Smith et al.,1997).

The psychological development of listening begins with someone's awareness of and attention to sounds or speech patterns (receiving), proceeds through identification and recognition of specific auditory signals (decoding), and ends in comprehension connection (understanding); the humanistic connections we make during a discussion or when someone walks by with a smile or frown. The concept of human connections and listening with love is the connections we have with one another on a metaphysical level i.e., on a spiritual level or the nature of being totally connected (Moore & Bruder, 1996). In other words, it is the connection human beings have, not only in the physical world, but also somewhere outside of it.

For example, I have had many women tell me that they could walk into a room and physically feel the atmosphere. They could feel the emotions of the people in the room. They could feel if it was a friendly or loving atmosphere or a room going through some form of tension. I have had students, both male and female, who told me, "I knew from day one that I was going to have a problem with that course." These individuals felt something outside of the physical world. They felt this without talking to the instructor or other students in the classroom. I have heard the following statement many times, "I could look at her and tell I wasn't going to like her." On the other hand, other individuals told me that he or she was wrong about their feelings. They stated that the person that they thought they would not like, or the course they felt poorly about turned-out to be the best thing that had ever happen to them. This means that often our perceptions about someone or something is often thwarted by preconceived notions and that's where discourse and research comes in.

In order for us to receive love and the gifts of life through the connectedness of human beings, we must first acknowledge the connection. Talk to someone about those feelings of connectedness or disconnect. Many times, feelings are a guide to something or someone who needs a gesture of love. Feelings and emotions can also be distorted creating a false sense of security. The instant we learn how to separate from the connection to those feelings and emotions, we can embrace the possibility of a perfect loving connection, or environment. I argue that alienating others through negative feelings, we are denying our own identity and destiny. In the metaphysical or spiritual realm, understand that you can create order from disorder, and preserve your destiny by understanding and controlling your emotions.

You must realize that in the metaphysical realm, reality is not purely the changes in feelings and emotions, but why they occur. That is the explanation of the forces that cause change. Specifically, when we are discussing human connections, the basic elements enter new combinations under two forces, love and strife, which are essentially forces of attraction and separation (Moore & Bruder, 1996).

By recognizing and listening to our feelings during human connections, the false impression of dislike, mistrust, and division could dissipate if we believe with true faith and we listen with love. We could actually recognize the potential in others. Learning to go beyond first characterizations and feelings, and embracing an ethical, moral, and learning way of thinking could dissipate any feelings of strife while embracing feelings of love. This is not to say that recognizing interconnectedness means abandoning boundaries. It is more than a point-of-view; it is a way of thinking that can greatly influence in subtle and covert ways that we are in fact love. The ideal of listening with love and interconnectedness is a way of being, rather than a skill or a tool to use within relationships, which may even be harmful if not used positively.

Understanding the mysteries of love and human beings, rather than assuming positive or negative knowledge, builds upon the relationship. The feelings we have are a predictor of a connection. However, living in the metaphysical or nature of being is the predictor of a 'successful' love connection. When we talk about a love connection it is holistic, not just physical, or social, or economical, it is spiritual. Let us say that the paradigm is considered to be a composition of interrelated, overlapping experiences and continuous processes. From reflecting on those experiences, we pick apart and alter those interactive human feelings, only seeing experiences in terms of isolated units. It is basically individual relativism, the theory that what is positive (and negative) is what you believe is positive (and negative) (Moore & Bruder, 1996). Recognizing interactions and the paradigm as a process that motivates a more holistic way of working through feelings of negativity is the first step. Interconnectedness exists on many levels from the relationship with education, to the power of thoughts, to the metaphysical realm of just being in love.

Taking into account the creative nature of the spirit is also applicable when considering the paradigm as a process; as humans embrace and accept the physical and the metaphysical world. Humans will produce and overcome through the physical world, thus creating a different metaphysical life, or nature of being; a "nature of being" that is encouraging, caring, compassionate, sensitive, and gentle. As each moment goes by, our lives are reinvented under that paradigm. If you think about it, you created your paradigm as it is today, you created your level of existence, you predicted it, and confirmed it through personal reflections and observations. The paradigm is a process just as our perception of love and relationships are both concurrently interconnected. Interconnectedness is related to the reasons people buy-in on change and development to the extent to which relationships live-up to their expectations. The following Courage Conviction Leadership Model (CCL) looks at the social value of interconnectedness. The model looks at managing and maintaining a balance between love and social order; by developing strategies where everyone wins through love.

Whether knowingly or otherwise, people live out of their reflections, and experiences. For example, novice students and faculty members at universities assimilate into their new environment initially from their experiences, and make their psychological, physical, and sociological adjustments. During those adjustments, the most important activities performed are their reactions during those introductory interactions with others. The value of the interactions with others will be weighted by the proactive responses to any environment and cultural norms.

Although, the traditions and norms may differ in terms of attitude toward specific issues such as equal opportunity, access, the social mission, and other implicit valuables – the underlining role of the individual is to examine the better match or comparison between personal philosophy, and the environment. The model illustrates how perceptions might be socially developed, or adjusted to the traditional policies, procedures, and philosophy. This contemporary analysis and philosophy is one that focuses on perceptions and more importantly on equal opportunities. This analysis is important because equal perceptions are the portal to social and political success. Can perceptions and experiences be intertwined and interwoven into a "nice-neat technique" of indifference and labeling? Yes, if monitored.

The method and model incorporates a form of identity socialization through "Paradigm Processing". According to Doob, (1994) "Socialization is a progression where participants are concerned with values and beliefs that are passed on to participants in that society, a process by which a person becomes a social being, learning the necessary cultural content and behavior to become a member of a group or society." The Socialization Method can be direct or indirect, verbal or nonverbal, overt or covert (Kuhn, 1962; Huene-Hoyningen, 1993; Dietze, 2001). The Socialization Paradigm Process transpires through the observation of modes, sequences, and styles of behavior during interactions with people.

Modeling of behaviors and exposure to culturally relevant material and activities are some of the methods stakeholders, in cultures, use to facilitate socialization through Paradigm Processing their values and beliefs. The critical process for those traditionalist stakeholders is the philosophies that hold personal historic values. The values and norms in cultures, societies, and communities are passed-on through education and spirituality. Specifically, the acquisition of wealth or success within the dominant culture that is associated with reputation, and traditional beliefs. Cultural beliefs and ideology, that controls who, what, where and how success is achieved (Dietze, 2001; Beauboeuf et el., 1996).

As stated earlier, Paradigm Processing occurs in human development throughout life stages; those life stages through developmental learning that cause a change in the self-identity of the person. In other words, "For every action there is an equal and opposite reaction" (Isaac Newton's Third Law). Newton's Third Law states that in every interaction in time, there is a pair of forces acting on the two interacting issues, concerns, or bodies. The aspect of the forces on the first interaction equals the aspect of the force on the second interaction. The direction of the force on the first interaction is contrary to the direction of the force on the second interaction. Forces continuously come in pairs – equal and opposite action-reaction force pairs (Born, 1975).

## Research/Resource

The third phase is the resource/research cycle of the 4R Model (Figure 3). Individuals internally or externally identify what has not been obtained through discussions. Whatever is not understood, unbelievable, and/or insubstantial is identified and researched to obtain information for change to occur. However, with research comes the need for resources, which is now in a union with traditions, norms, and values.

For instance, a friend of mine was interested in starting his own business. He didn't have the funds to start a business and his credit wasn't the best. When he did not hear about any programs that would help him do what he envisioned doing, he did his own research. He researched buildings that were up for donation to non-for-profit programs, and grants to fund his objectives. I wrote and submitted his corporate papers and bylaws to the Secretary of State. He eventually found a grant that would get him started, and an organization that would house his support programs.

As his responsibility for continued learning, how to improve his non-for-profit business shifts to independent thinking, and to the individual participant/learner, the emphasis of the process of help those individuals shifts. Thus getting closer to a total Paradigm Shift, where growth is continual. According to Dohmen (cited in Knapper & Cropley,

2000), the concept of learning includes, "independent thinking, decision making and acceptance of responsibility."

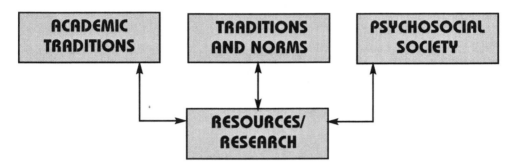

**FIGURE 3.** *Resources/Research*

**(Read Aloud)**
**Everything that I do will add to my credibility as a positive force in the lives of those around me, by living earnestly.**

If he or she does not take notice of the signs that clearly indicate that he or she is unprepared, then he or she should prepare for their credibility to be challenged. For instance, the *American Idol* Television show has only one winner out of many thousands that show-up. Many losers of the *American Idol* did not know or believe that he or she could not sing. They really believed in their dream and traveled from city to city trying-out over-and-over again just to be judged and denied. All of them were in denial; yet, living in faith. Many of them lost more than a chance to be the next singing star, they lost credibility among those who sponsored them financially, emotionally, and psychologically because when they had to stand in front of people who were considered professionals in the field, they found out that they really could not sing.

If people are telling you that, "you cannot sing," you probably cannot sing, but because you believed so deeply in yourself, you were able to convince people to believe in you too. Unfortunately, when you are surrounded by others who are not really invested in you or are seeking the same opportunity as you, you may be forced to face the harsh reality. What will this teach you?

I ask such an absurd question. Does an "embarrassing moment," such as what could happen on the *American Idol,* equate to a learning experience? Another question is, how do we make every experience one where positive learning takes place earnestly? Living earnestly requires that we have the ability to listen to the claims that produce compelling convictions about our abilities on the side of common sense and truth – even if it hurts.

I believe that there is only one way of living for people, and that is to stroke the fires of enthusiasm for life. Which is what I think those who audition for the *American Idol* are engaged in; an enthusiasm for life. The hopeful decided one day to take a chance on themselves. The key here is to try. You may or may not fail, but what if you never try. You will spend your entire life wondering "what if?" And what a terrible way to live your life; constantly wondering if you could have been the next *American Idol*. All you have to do is step out on faith. Say that you are going to win and believe it. Not everyone walks away with a million dollar record deal; but they all gain the peace in knowing that they gave their dream a chance.

Daniel Hale Williams was the first African-American to perform heart surgery. A pioneer in the field, he performed surgery on a man who had suffered a stab wound to the chest. Without x-rays, blood transfusions, or anesthetics, he opened the man's chest with the help of a surgical team and repaired the wound. With time being of the essence, he didn't have time to be afraid. He knew what needed to be done. Please note that this event took place in 1893, a time when African-Americans were still fighting for equality, still trying to break barriers, and perceptions that considered them inferior – let alone intelligent enough to perform such a complex procedure, but he believed in himself and in his ability to save the man's life so passionately that others in the room did not question it.

You must stroke the flames of change in order to take control of your life for personal growth and fulfillment, and that is the essence of Paradigm Processing. It is important that we live earnest and honestly for real growth and fulfillment. So that when we have the opportunity to show-off our uniqueness you know without a doubt that you are the best and no matter what anyone says, you will go that extra mile to prove it.

## Responsibility

This leads to the fourth and final R (Figure 4); Responsibility to the community. The application of this model is the explicit sharing of knowledge and information. Depending on the norms and values, learning in the end gives the recipient a sense of responsibility to think in broad concepts such as for the common good, and the willingness to give back. If you give back, you will get back physically and metaphysically. I recall one morning, I received a text message from my niece in-law saying, "Today is Aunt Jackie's 60th birthday, and I want everyone to call her and wish her a happy birthday." I thought to myself, if Aunt Jackie was a giving person, a person who regularly gave of her time, her support, gave to the community, gave at her job, at church, or gave to her family, this text message would not be necessary. Everyone remembers a person who gives.

Because Aunt Jackie decided to live in isolation, to live without a giving spirit, and in her constricting reflections, her ability to receive was limited. Responsibility or giving back starts with the first "R", Reflection. Responsibility is the beginning of reflecting consciously and unconsciously, because as you give back more information, more thoughts, and more ideas are created (see Figure 5). What one learns in the context of the situation is applied consciously or unconsciously to the social and cultural world. In other words, "for every positive action there is an equal and opposite reaction" – an emotion, a willingness to return the favor in some kind of way.

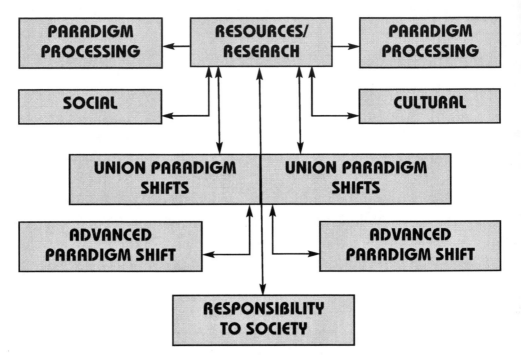

**FIGURE 4.** *Responsibility*

During the model, Paradigm Processing is leading to a complete and holistic Paradigm Shift. Paradigm Processing is continually affecting perception and experience. With Paradigm Processing in the 4R Model, the connection or union of information causes a complete Paradigm Shift. This new paradigm is believed to cause a humanistic social responsibility effect, absolutely and unequivocally, to the community. The 4R Model creates an understanding in the practice of transformation and transition by creating an individual's ability to positively contribute to the world. The ideology is that participants want to understand perceptional development from Paradigm Processing whether it be education, professional, or personal.

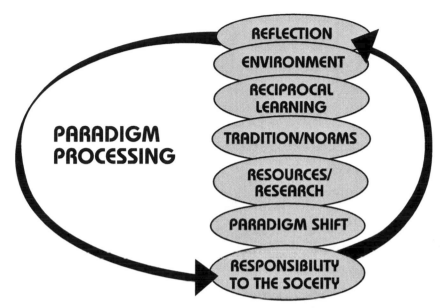

**FIGURE 5.** *4R, Paradigm Processing Perception Model*
*© William A. Martin, 2004*

The proactive factors of the model are the total Paradigm Shifts toward the betterment of the individual, the institution of education, business, and society.

**(Read Aloud)**
**I am in control of my life!**

It's your life and you must take control of it. You cannot blame anyone for your current status in life. When you blame others for the problems in your life, you give up all control or the ability to solve them. Do you want to do that? So much time is wasted on trying to figure out who is to blame than what can we do to fix what's wrong. No matter who's to blame, you have to take responsibility for your life. Do not waste precious time on people who hinder your growth. Do not expend the energy on negative thoughts and negative people. Nothing happens in your life unless you allow it to happen. If you don't like where you are in life, it is your responsibility to change things. Seek a favorable outcome to some of the unresolved issues in your life. The past is called the past for a reason. Don't waste your time thinking about yesterday – create a new today.

**(Read Aloud)**
**I will be a faithful giver!**

The 4R Model was deliberately designed to focus on topics ranging from broad theoretical concepts; concepts that are spiritual, and faith-base, experiential, educational, and knowledge based. The results connect knowledge, basic individualized ideology, and discourse, which encourage a well-balanced society, and community. The model and the process is about preventative knowledge, perceptions, connections, relationships, and discourse that sustain you in faith and in the physical.

According to Knapper & Cropley (2000), the concept is anticipatory knowledge – knowledge that can be used in novel situations, not anticipated by anyone or an emphasized goal. In other words, the goal is to maintain the faith, and anything outside of that goal is unacceptable, that includes practical or new knowledge. Lindeman, (1961), believed that, "Knowledge leads to power; power leads to self-expression, freedom and creativity." Daley purported, "New knowledge is made meaningful by the ways in which learners establish connections between knowledge learned, previous experiences, and the context in which learners find themselves" (Daley, 2001). People in general, are continuingly reflecting on previous experiences. The individual cherishes those experiences in reflection; however, the external person or group does not cherish it or find it important unless it relates to them.

# Chapter 2

*Before observing, envision the
likelihood given the conditions.*

The 4R Paradigm Processing Model is predicated on Bayes' Theorem, where Paradigm Processing becomes a Paradigm Shift. According to Anderson et al., (1996), Bayes' theorem is used extensively in decision analysis. The prior probabilities are often subjective estimates provided by a decision maker. Sample information is obtained and posterior probabilities are computed for use in developing a decision strategy. For example, I remember my brother had a defining moment in his life. He had to decide whether he was going to the Vietnam War or going to college. I remember he had just met his girlfriend, Veronica, and his grades where shaky at best. The prior probability was that he would be called to combat and maybe killed. His culture, African-American, and the climate, the civil rights movement, did not indicate that the armed forces would benefit him at all.

The information that we heard on the daily news indicated that hundreds of Americans were being killed every month. My brother did his research, found some resources, and made it his responsibility to finish high school with a Grade-Point-Average that would get him into a quality university. He figured that if he became a social being within his high school, all the things he needed would come to him. He volunteered to serve at school events, church events and meetings. He did everything that his pastor, teachers, and administration wanted him to do and more. By going that extra mile, his posterior probabilities were conducive to his needs for that time, place, and space in history.

# Chapter 3

*Building a life of joy requires an under-
standing of who we are inside in proportion to what others see on the
outside and the historical consequence.*

I think it is important that I personalize Paradigm Processing first so
that you can have a real world example of where the ideology started.
When I first completed the requirements for my doctorate degree, I
thought that it would be the beginning of me earning lots and lots of
money. Well, that did not happen, initially. What did happen was a
change in my thought process. I had envisioned myself earning my
Bachelors, Masters, and Doctorate degrees, and I went out and worked
hard to achieve those goals. However, the money I thought I would
receive after completing my education did not come.

I remember the day I told my son that I had completed my doctorate. I said, "I am finished, I completed my doctorate program." He
turned his head and looked at me with a weird expression on his face.
With a confused look on his face, he said, "Dad, did you ever see yourself as a millionaire?" That question confused me, but it also aroused my
intellect. Everything that I had done in my life, I had envisioned it in my
mind by Paradigm Processing my thoughts and dreams until their
completion. I had envisioned something and I made it happen with
discourse, faith, and hard work. I thought to myself, "Why not envision
myself becoming wealthy and making that come true?" Therefore, I
did. After changing my vision to become wealthy, within one month,

with property investments, I began to work toward that vision. I had Paradigm Processed my visions of earning my degrees, and now I was well on the way to Paradigm Processing my way to financial wealth.

The content of Paradigm Processing occurs in human development throughout life stages. It is contextualized throughout the stages of lifelong learning; that learning that causes changes in one's self-identity, whether it is learned directly, indirectly, formally, or informally. The ideology of Paradigm Processing was developed and written to help people realize how their discourse with others, faith, spirituality, is the key to finishing anything that they put their minds to.

# Chapter 4

*In order for you to grow to your full potential, you must believe in yourself and feel worthy of your vision. You have to feel that you deserve success.*

How? You gain confidence by concentrating on the talents and attributes that make you special and unique; it is that thing that you were called to do, that thing that you take for granted, like cooking, catching fish, speaking, motivating, encouraging, or telling jokes. Like all experiences in life, understanding that Paradigm Processing your vision of holistic wealth is a philosophy that says, "Do what you do best, and do that thing that brings you joy." It is a philosophy of motivating, and encouraging personal growth in the spiritual, social, and economic areas; a process of growth through positive thinking and acting – acting with true faith toward success. Over-time and throughout this process of growth, you are building a vision brick-by-brick, step-by-step, bringing you closer to your goal. Eventually, your vision of holistic wealth will come true as well, but first, you must feel worthy of success.

**(Read Aloud)**
**I will take control of my life; express my uniqueness for personal growth and fulfillment.**

Throughout this book, I stress the importance of feeling deeply and passionate about your vision, goals, and God-given uniqueness; that uniqueness that is in your DNA, just like your bone structure, or hair color the things that you were born with it. However, unless you are emotionally and physically involved in your uniqueness, you cannot expect your dreams and goals to come true. For example, a very successful musician wrote about how he taught himself to play the guitar. He started playing at the age of 17 years old, which is late for most musicians. He talked about how he knew inside that he was a musician, but never took his talent seriously. He stated that at an early age he could hear when instruments and voices were off-pitch when others could not.

This reflecting on his musical talents started with his research on how to become a professional musician. He began by listening to the most well known bands in the world. He stated that he focused specifically on the electric guitar solos. After he listened to the solos over 10 times, he would practice to the point where he would get sick. He practiced day and night, but most importantly, he talked about his vision, and was not afraid to pull out his guitar at any occasion. He was passionate about his life, his vision, and found joy in living in that moment.

The point here is that talent without a vision, passion, or joy will never see the light of day. Obviously, sports would be a good example; if you have a vision about your life that is exciting to you because of the uniqueness of your skills with it, such as singing, art, or recreational pursuit, joy will follow. On the other hand, although we all have uniqueness, the ones who are earnest in their beliefs with reflection, and have the persuasiveness in finding people to help with their goals will truly find joy. No matter what, the process is good; because without knowing where your uniqueness is, you will never find true joy.

**(Read Aloud)**
**I will be an enthusiastic force without fear.**

The best method of reaching your dreams is to have a dogmatic determination about your goals. You must continue to grow in your efforts by throwing your heart into the cause you create for yourself. You must take every opportunity to have discourse with others about your goals. Stand up and assert yourself at public meetings when it is about your goals, if only to acknowledge your existence and place in that spatial environment. You have but to look around to see that your experiences can help someone, or allow you to continue to grow through someone else's experiences. You never know what progress you can make unless you engage people in discourse repeatedly about your needs.

As I write this book, I am continually growing educationally wealthy myself. I know and have seen enough, through lecturing, counseling, and advising students in higher education, and motivational speaking, to know that whatever your problems are, they are not unique. For example, many adult students that I have spoken to have stated that historically they hated taking mathematic courses, yet, it has always been a requirement for a higher education degree. To get those people through those fears of enrolling in advance mathematic courses, the first thing I tell them to do is to stop saying that they hate mathematics. Once you say that you hate something you close your mind to the possibility, which controls and leads your paradigm in a negative direction. After that, I told those fearful people to say to themselves, "What one person can do, another person can do. Just as the multitude of individuals who were afraid of taking mathematics and passed anyway to earn their higher education degrees, so can I." My job and yours is to build confidence while allowing others to let go of their historical negative past.

While others will hold on to their problems, you will learn how to put them in their rightful place in history, to contextualize and reconstruct them. Additionally, as others discuss the problems in their history, you should choose not to do so unless it will help another person learn from it. While many labor remorselessly to get pass those educational and psychological walls, you will learn how to achieve goals with ease.

This means that you have to cherish your vision, see yourself in your vision, and live in your vision. However, first you must start to measure and match your naturally given talents to your vision.

Next, strive to find something in your life that you truly enjoy, that you would do for free or for the mere pleasure of it, and find a way to get paid for it. For example, every basketball player in the National Basketball Association (NBA) would play basketball without being paid for it. However, they get paid to showcase the talents that they where naturally born with. All of them went through stages of growth to get to the level of professional basketball player. Most of them were born with natural abilities to play basketball, and the rest of them just had faith, worked hard, and did not give-up on their dream.

I remember when I had a vision of playing professional basketball. I would go outside everyday and practice with anyone who was willing to play with a novice like myself. During this period in my life, I met many excellent basketball players who had the same vision of becoming a professional player. However, one-day, I met a young man who was my age, and in my class, who had the same vision as me. He introduced me to professional basketball when we started attending the Chicago Bulls games together. We would go watch Chet Walker and Bob Love play. My friend's name is Eddie Johnson (Piggy). He later played professional basketball in Houston, Texas, and Kansas City, Kansas.

**(Read aloud)**
**I will have power over my life.**

In my journey here, I have seen and met many people like Eddie Johnson, who worked hard to achieve their vision. On the other hand, I have also seen and met many more people working hard to maintain, what I consider, a form of "slavery." People working in areas that has destroyed their vision of happiness, vision of joy, and continue to destroy the essence of their individual identity. They are guaranteed to maintain their present status, which preserves their limited level of happiness and condition. I caught the whiff of the "working dead" early in life, but it became more prominent during my presentations, and listening to adult students who spoke of their current status in life.

During this period in my life, prior to earning my degrees, it was those individuals that I met in the early mornings waiting for the bus to go to their place of employment. Day-in and day-out, I would see the same faces. They did not look happy. I often asked myself, "Is this where I want to end up?" They were among the many reasons my mind changed from just working to exist, to working at something that would bring me joy. I knew that in order to change my life, I had to change my paradigm, or my mindset. I had to have the faith to burn all of the bridges behind me in order to become holistically wealthy (i.e., physically and mentally healthy, socially and spiritually aware). Burning all of the bridges behind me did not mean letting go of those positive and productive relationships, but releasing all fears, "speaking power, speaking wealth, and speaking freedom" into my life, while "tearing down the walls" of negativity through true faith and the belief that I was doing the right thing; not just for me, but for everyone around me.

First, let me say that I am in no way saying that just being monetarily successful is the desire of most adults. I am talking about those individuals who have not lost faith in the idea of becoming "holistically" wealthy through better education, through spiritual inheritance, through having fun and learning to enjoy their lives, and through hard work.

At all cost, I became determined to learn from others who had become wealthy. I started researching the quickest means to economic wealth, while increasing my faith and the joy of life. I began to read books written by people who had conquered their fears, to live their vision and dreams of wealth. Just as I had been formally educated to fit society's status quo, I was teaching myself to live above the majority who worked to maintain the minimum standard of living. One of the issues that have always come up throughout my experiences as a student, adult educator, counselor, and advisor, is that adults go back to school to increase their standards of life physically, economically and socially.

I really enjoy talking to adult students, because adults have that wisdom that differentiates facts from fiction. It also helps with teaching, because they can interject with more experiences than the younger undergraduate student. For instance, I teach others to embrace their happiness, to enjoy life, to become self-motivated, to speak power, and wealth into their lives. I teach them to construct a paradigm that "tears down the walls" between the dimensions of success. Adult students find it easier to receive these messages due to their journey that has brought them to their current place in life.

When I was younger, like most young people, I was not living a holistically wealthy life, I had to seize the moment and take control of my paradigm – and my existence. I also knew that I had to release the fear of becoming wealthy. As we will see later, unless that fear is crucial to your survival at that time, place, and space, fear is the single largest cause for failure. I had to start to think differently about everything in my life – my relationships, my goals, and my approach to the things that mattered. I had to seize control of all of my responsibilities by realizing that time is too short and if I wanted to be happy, I had to utilize each minute – each second as if it was my last to refurbish my faith, my spirit, and my life.

# Chapter 5

*How do we Paradigm Process positively in the midst of chaos? How do we deal proactively with challenges that life throws at us to overcome and live a life of joy and wealth. Resolving that impossibility requires something like an evolutionary change of who we are, how we behave, how we think, and what we value in our life.*

Due to my childhood economic status, I have lived in some of the most dangerous areas of Chicago's west and south sides. I have lived around pimps, prostitutes, drug dealers, gangs, and addicts. Illegal transactions were part of the norm. I was exposed to the deterioration of communities, gang violence, and the disenfranchisement of those individuals who unfortunately were to serve as my role models. From those experiences, I have found that most of the individuals, who are involved in illegal acts, in that narrow sub-cultural environment, are perceived as being "successful." It is a culture where success is measured by tailor-made clothes, custom-painted cars, money, the number of children, and how many beautiful women you had. That was the image of success, unfortunately. From a social psychological perspective, the successful people in the community influenced the way the other people, especially the young people, thought and learned and this varied by community and cultural group. Many behaviorist psychologists believe that learning requires a natural setting. They believe that young children imitated those around them as part of their learning process (Smaldino, 2008).

I was born in Chicago Illinois, Henry Horner Homes; a Chicago Housing Authority (CHA) subsidized housing projects. My family and I lived there until my seventh birthday. At that time, there were seven of us in my family, my father, my mother, my two brothers, and my two sisters. I was the youngest male of three. At that time in my life, I thought that I was living in the best neighborhood in Chicago. While living in the projects, I had my first experience with death. I was walking up the stairs when I saw a boy running down the stairs. I remember it vividly like it happened yesterday. A boy was walking down the brick stairs with a bag of pop bottles, which he was returning to the store for ten cents per bottle. He had several bags. I looked at him and said, "What's up?" He looked at me as he ran pass. After walking up about two floors, I heard the sound of glass breaking, screams, and calls for help. By the time, I got back down the stairs there were people running around everywhere. Blood was everywhere. I ran home in shock; devastated by what I had just witnessed. He was dead and I was the last person he spoke to. I couldn't understand this. He was so young. I remember standing over him as the blood formed a pool around him and he took his last breath. I wondered what he was thinking at that time. I wondered if he would take the memory of me with him to Heaven or to the place that God had chosen for him. As I contemplated all of this, I asked myself what was I supposed to learn from that experience. A discourse that only lasted a few seconds, had such a lasting impact on me. I often wonder if that moment, that discourse, was to teach me that life is too short and that no matter who we meet in our journey of life it must be handled with great importance and responsibility because we may never have an opportunity to have it again.

Practice: Think about a moment when a complete stranger stopped to talk to you and it left a lasting impact on your life.

Share that moment here:

_____

_____

_____

_____

_____

_____

_____

_____

_____

When I was eight years old, my family and I moved for the first of many times to 'K' town, which is located on the west side of Chicago. This area was on the down swing of economic depression. It was there that I earned my first pair of All Star gym shoes from my mother. At ten dollars, they were the most expensive gym shoes you could buy. They were so nice that when you got a pair, you did not wear them on the ground for fear of getting them dirty, they were only worn on the gym floor.  To protect them and keep them looking new, I tied the shoes strings together and put them over my shoulder so that everyone could see them. I remember the first day I did that, one of the gang members in the area snatched them right off of my back. We struggled for a while, until he stopped, looked at me, and said, "Do you want to die for these gym shoes?" I let go and they were gone. After that incident it was back to the Pro Keds, the shoes that all of my friends laughed at and I hated. At that moment, two things could have happened. I could have chosen to be tough to avoid the embarrassment that walking away without putting up a fight could have caused. I could have walked away to avoid the ongoing ridicule that my assumed cowardice could have caused amongst my peers. With only seconds to make the decision of a life-time, I chose to walk away. Interesting enough, what I feared did not happen, but instead not only did I gain a renewed sense of respect for myself, but my friends did not ridicule me; gaining their respect and the reverence of others who were told the story. What I learned in that moment is that although you can put a price on material things, you cannot put a price on life, and when those Pro Keds became worn and tattered, I would still be here years later stronger and wiser because of that lesson.

Practice: Have you ever found yourself in a moment where the choice was life or death? What were you thinking in that moment and do you think that you made the right decision and why?

Share that moment here:

_____

_____

_____

_____

_____

_____

_____

_____

_____

_____

When I was eleven years old, I started working with my grandfather at the gas station he managed, while my family continued their move around the Chicago-land area. My family and I moved to the Austin Neighborhood. We lived right across the street from Austin High School, which had an open space with a basketball court, baseball field, and an area where we could play football. Self-taught, I learned to play every one of those sports extremely well. Although living in this area gave me great joy it was also a time of great turmoil. My mother and father fought often. With seven mouths to feed, there was never enough. Having to choose between keeping a roof over our heads or putting food on the table caused a rift between my parents. As a result, my father was forced to leave the home several times, leaving us worst off. Soon after my father left, we moved again, eight more times to be exact bringing the total of moves to seventeen times before the age of eighteen. Watching this discourse between my parents may have inadvertently assisted in my development of male and female relationships. The constant anger shared over not having enough drove me to strive for opportunities that wouldn't create a sense of lack and a sense in knowing through everything good and bad there must be a discourse that creates bonds of longevity and respect.

Practice: Think about a time when you were involved in a heated argument. There were probably things that were said and/or done in anger. Looking back could you have done anything differently that could have resulted in a different outcome?

Share that moment here:

_____

_____

_____

_____

_____

_____

_____

_____

_____

_____

The day my father left was a day that is still ingrained in my mind. I remember I was coming in from playing basketball one day. As I walked through the door, I saw my brothers holding my father's arms like the police taking a prisoner to their police van. As they walked down the stairs, I could hear my mother yelling, "Get out!" As they walked him out of our house, I walked out with them to watch my father walk down the street with nowhere to go. That was a defining moment in my life. I was in conflict. I couldn't understand what was happening to me - to our family. I loved my mother, but I didn't understand why my father had to leave. We struggled, but we always had each other. I began to act out. I was angry and did not know how to express it. The very next day, I started cursing. I had never intentionally cursed before that day. It was a dark time for me. It was not long before I saw my father again and although he no longer stood as head of our household, he took his role as father seriously. He started bringing food to the house, mailing money, and making sure that he was still in his children's lives.

After he left, we continued to move from apartment to apartment. We lived in buildings that should have been abandoned. Some of the places we lived in did not have hot water, plumbing, or heat. The good thing was that my mother did not let us believe that we were poor or at least I did not know it. I only saw the positive and was very grateful that my family was still together, and that we ate every day.

Practice: What does sacrifice mean to you? What is the one thing that you cannot live without and why? Please note that the answer to this question cannot focus on tangible things like a 42 inch television, a cellphone, or a car.

Share that moment here:

_____

_____

_____

_____

_____

_____

## Speak Power, Speak Wealth and Speak Freedom

_____

_____

_____

_____

_____

_____

# Chapter 6

*Praise, encouragement, and
motivation starts at "home".*

My mother was the first motivational speaker in my life. I remember when my mother took me to register for pre-school classes. My mother and two teachers took me into a classroom for an examination. Later, I found out that examination was an I.Q. test. They sat me down and put a puzzle in front of me, and asked me to put the puzzle together as quickly as possible. They turned away to talk and when they looked back the puzzle was complete and I was playing with some other toys in the area. They talked to my mother and soon after, she came over to me and whispered in my ear. She said, "Artwell, you are a genius." Now, I did not hear that from the teachers who issued the test. Nevertheless, I took that to heart. My mother had a way of making me feel special, important, smart, and proud. No matter what we were going through, she always praised and encouraged all of her children's intellect and curiosity.

Practice: My mother's words influenced me to become the man that I am today. Who influenced you and how?

Share that moment here:

_____

_____

_____

_____

_____

_____

_____

_____

_____

_____

_____

Even through all of that turmoil, I went on to earn my Undergraduate and Graduate Degrees from Chicago State University. My under-graduate concentration was in Geography and Economics. My Master's Degree is in Geography with a concentration in Economic Development and Geographical Information Systems (GIS). I completed my formal education at Northern Illinois University (NIU), earning my Doctorate of Education, concentrating in Adult, Counseling, and Higher Educa-tion. I have owned businesses, investment stocks, and investment property. All of the things I have done and accomplished started with one thing and one thing only, and that was a "mental" vision, followed by faith, and then the willingness to take risks.

# Chapter 7

*When you freely give of yourself, give from the heart; give unconditionally. To give unconditionally is to know that there may never be any "thank you(s)" or rewards, but only the satisfying feeling of knowing that you have helped someone.*

Philanthropy is one of the keys to mental and physical success. Mentally, giving back touches the soul of the human spirit, and helps to build relationships. Physically, giving back to the community and the environment without expectance helps to eliminate stress, and physically connects those who have monetary advantages to those less fortunate. I give back in so many ways to my community; whether it is giving money to my local church, or donating clothes to the homeless. I am also the founder and board member of the Srewolf & Nitram Foundation H.E.A.R.T.S. (Helping, Ex-offenders, and Addicts Return to Society). The goal of the foundation is to help those individuals who did their time in prison and were rehabilitated to find housing and programs that would improve their lives holistically.

I also started volunteering in the community as a baseball coach, which involves buying equipment, setting up games with other community volunteers, practices, picking up my players and delivering equipment to various destinations. In other words, as a philanthropist, community volunteer, and believer in reciprocal spiritual faith, I contribute to an individual's and the community's well-being.

In October of 2008, Mr. Epstein, a philanthropist, contacted Project H.O.M.E. and offered a challenge to its donors and hopefully new donors in the community: if Project H.O.M.E. was able to raise $25,000 in only one month, he would generously match those funds dollar for dollar. Mr. Epstein is an example of the type of creative fundraising charities need in a tough economic climate. He is an example to others in the community who can, despite pinched purses make a big impact in their community. Mr. Epstein took the idea of a $25,000 gift and made it an even more meaningful $50,000 gift with the great efforts of the collective community (Project H.O.M.E. 2009).

Mr. Epstein obviously believed in reciprocal giving and faith. He has the belief that what you give is what you get. The thing is, you do not go into giving expecting to receive. You go into giving just with the expectation of feeling good about giving, and rejuvenating your community and your faith.

# Chapter 8

*"Success is not the key to happiness. Happiness is the key to success. If you love what you are doing, you will be successful."*

**Albert Schweitzer**

Throughout my experiences, I found that most people work in areas that do not bring them holistic happiness and joy. For those adults working in an area that does not bring happiness and joy to their life, he or she is not only losing valuable time, they are also in the process of becoming mentally, socially, and economically impoverished. In other words, their hopes, goals, and dreams began to diminish and dissolve in their efforts over-time. Also, from my experiences, most adults are dependent on a job or work that bring them stress, which as many adults have told me, "It is not fulfilling," and lacks healthy growth.

Most of the people that I have come in contact with during my life have at one time or another wanted to be wealthy. Most have said that, "Early on in life, I thought of becoming a millionaire, but as time went on those thoughts disappeared." In short, 99.9% stated that through too many negative employment transitions, they have felt the urge to go for their goals and dreams that they believe would have brought joy to their life, wealth, personal growth, and fulfillment, but life dictated something else. Unhealthy growth for the working adult is especially noticed during times of transition; issues that adults deal with on a daily basis like work, children, personal life, and family health issues.

This ideology of Paradigm Processing is useful for the young and older person who may believe that it is too late to live their vision of success, their dreams of earning a degree, wealth, and goals for their family. Paradigm Processing will bring great wealth to you and to the future generations of your family. My method is simple. Anyone can use it, but it is particularly excellent for the adult who believes that it is too late to be successful and happy. What you do after reading this book will reflect on the person you are creating for yourself in the future. Paradigm Processing is about creating a future where you have control of your spiritual, social, emotional, and physical self.

## Spiritual
- Take up a worthy cause
- Do volunteer work
- Trust God
- Give thanks
- Use prayer
- Worship with others
- Follow religious traditions
- Meditate
- Take a stand on your values
- Enjoy nature's beauty

## Social
- Build good family relationships
- Express affection, give hugs
- Maintain family traditions
- Meet new neighbors
- Share compliments
- Make use of community organizations – join clubs
- Let people know what you need

- Share your problems and ask for support
- SMILE!

## Emotional

- Believe in yourself
- Treat yourself to something special
- Look at the good side of things
- Plan for the future
- Do not let things pile up
- Ask for help when you need it
- Use your sense of humor
  (tell a joke, watch a funny television show, etc.)
- Learn something new
- Take a class
- Listen to music and sing
- Play a game
- Tackle a new project
- Keep busy

## Physical

- Listen to your body and know your limits
- Exercise, walk, swim, and dance
- Eat nutritious meals
- Get enough sleep
- Take a warm, relaxing bath
- Tense and relax each muscle
- Take short stretch breaks thoughout your day
- Follow your doctor's orders
- Pamper yourself at the beauty shop (new hairstyle, manicure, etc.)
- Take a few deep breaths

# Chapter 9

*Embrace the talents that*
*make you who you are.*

With Paradigm Processing, I have outlined a number of positive and negative differences among people, and I take these differences and make them bigger, better, and useful to you and to society. I am talking about the differences or talents that make you who you are, that make you:

- **the singer that everyone wants to hear,**
- **the dancer that everyone wants to see,**
- **the writer whose work that everyone wants to read,**
- **the counselor that everyone wants to talk to, or**
- **the teacher that everyone wants to learn from.**

Although we know we have these talents and gifts, because of fear, dread, and faithlessness most of us never turn these talents into life sustaining work. The idea is that you should let go of the fear and realize your vision and dreams by giving your full attention to something you love and enjoy doing. According to Don Miguel Ruiz, "Death is not the biggest fear we have; our biggest fear is taking the risk to be alive, and express what we really are." Eleanor Roosevelt stated, "You gain strength, courage, and confidence by every experience in which you really stop to look fear in the face. You must do the thing, which you think you cannot do." Understanding your fears is the first step to obtaining the passion of life.

Now, I know that it is easier said than done. Fears are valid and not easy to overcome. The first step would be to identify what you are really afraid of and then attempt (notice that I said "attempt") to face it. Of course, you are going to experience an overwhelming feeling of anxiety and a strong urge to walk away, but think about how great you are going to feel once you get through the experience. You have to believe that you are capable of doing great things and achieving great mental, physical, economical, and emotional prosperity.

Practice: What is the one thing that you are afraid of that keeps you from achieving your goals. List it and then examine ways to overcome it.

Share your thoughts here:

_____

_____

_____

_____

_____

_____

_____

_____

_____

# Chapter 10

*At the right time, place, and space,*
*some men/women will break records,*
*while others will break.*

Some years ago, I lived in a poor to middle class neighborhood of Chicago. I was very athletic and active in the neighborhood. I remember meeting a young man who lived about three blocks away who, like me, loved to play all sports. Some of my new friends played with me regularly or others like this young man, played with me occasionally. One day, we were playing and he and I got into a fight. I punched him in the nose and it started bleeding badly. People closest to us broke the fight up, he went his way, and I went my way. As long as we had been playing together before that fight, like many other altercations, I thought that would be the end of it. I never saw him again, until twenty years later at the university's stairs where I was working and attending.

When I first saw him, I ran up and asked, "How are you doing." Before, I could get, "How are you doing?" out of my mouth, he ran up the university's stairs screaming, "I am 36 years old now, leave me alone!" I never saw him again on campus after that moment. Later, I thought to myself, why would he run away like that? I think he had been carrying that experience in his thoughts for over 20 years. Still afraid, still stuck in time, space, and in place of an event that ended in one person's mind and was relived over and over again in another. It was Isaac Newton who came to the conclusion that there is an absolute space and an absolute time. He stated that, "Time flows equably without regard to anything external; This is called duration" (Born, 1972). Newton also believed that absolute space, without regard to anything external, remains always similar and immoveable. He looked at place as something measurable to the person; it has personal value.

To understand how time, place, and space works, we need to spend some time thinking about how people turn a space into a place. One reason that it can be hard to see the division between place and space is that, in our everyday experiences, places largely exist within spaces. A place is generally a space with something added like a social meaning, resolution i.e., resolution to a fist fight, cultural understandings about position, events and natural history and so on. The impression of place converts the space. As a space, a large university is uninviting; but it is valued as a place for social interactions, research, and development. It is still a space, even though place is what matters. A place is where Paradigm Processing occurs.

Paradigm Processing is also based on Hume's empirical thought of knowledge and how by nature, we as human beings build foundations of thought (Hume, 1777). Our thoughts are not simply an assortment of perceptions, with nothing tying them together other than time and experience. Paradigm Processing is our thoughts along with discourse that link and connect similar thought foundations. It connects thoughts to the physical and the future, it moves through space and across time. For example, when you say to someone, "I was just talking about you and out of nowhere you called..." Or, the person you were talking about shows-up a couple of hours later or even the next day. Over-time, the discourse that you were having about that person that called or "showed-up" was a physical impression imbedded in space that traveled through space over-time and manifesting itself into the physical.

Albert Einstein proved that time is relative. Therefore, when we experience this philosophy of Paradigm Processing your future and time becomes truly relative. When we talk about someone and he or she calls or shows-up, the time that it took is relative because they always show-up. It is the same thing with the wealthiest people in the world, they talk about wealth, envision wealth, and wealth manifests itself in the physical. The only thing between you and wealth is time. Einstein proved that one person is able to experience several days while another person simultaneously experiences only a few hours or minutes. The same two people can meet up again, one having experienced days or even years while the other has only experienced minutes (Pais, 1982).

For instance, let us take a look at the lives of three young men who are friends from the same neighborhood, and they all go in different directions after high school. One stays home with his parents, another goes to the military, and the last one attends a university. After four years, the friend that attended the university graduates and has a job waiting for him. The friend that enlisted into the military comes back to town to attend the university four years behind his friend. The friend living at home with his parents has to go to the military because without any professional training, he will have to accept a job that doesn't pay him enough to put a roof over his head. Thereby, putting him socially and economically eight years behind his friend that attended the university, and four years behind the friend that enlisted into the military. Another example, the friend that stayed home with his parents could become a self-made millionaire, while his friends that came home from the military and graduated from a university will now seek employment from him. Time has become relative and in both situations resulting in a different cause and effect. It all depends on Paradigm Processing future events through time. All three of the friends where effected by the place they were in, but through time and space their paradigms where processed until a shift occurred to move to the next experience. The paradigm of friend that stayed home with his parents has been processed to become a millionare; thereby creating a vision of him becoming a millionare – whether it occurred when his friends came back, or just after they left, in time he was going to be wealthy.

Think of it like this, you are looking at an airplane 30,000 feet in the sky. The airplane looks like it is almost staying still, but it is not. Now you see an airplane at 20,000 feet and it looks like it is moving faster across the sky but they are traveling at the same speed. Now you see a third airplane landing and it looks like it is moving faster than the other two, but it is actually traveling slower. Each airplane is relative to each other through time, the faster they travel, the slower their time will pass relative to someone planted firmly on the earth. If they were able to travel at the speed of light, their time would cease completely and they would only exist trapped in timelessness. This is also true with Paradigm Processing, however in order to achieve great success in your life you must not exist trapped in timelessness, you have to move with time, around time and believe it before time. You have to get up and make things happen. You have to take steps to improve your life. You have to "speak power, speak wealth, and speak freedom" in order for a Paradigm Shift to occur.

Paradigm Processing, "tearing down the walls", has a provision of space and place. Think of it as an office that incorporates all of the newest machinery, such as, audio, and video equipment and computer technology. The equipment would supply a valuable, impressionable infrastructure for communication across time and space. Paradigm Processing occurs over-time, which as we know now is relative, and with active participation, a sense of place begins to sort through all those barriers to a Paradigm Shift. In regards to the machinery, the sense of place must be forged by the office workers and it cannot be instinctive in the organization itself.

Space is the opportunity and place is the understood reality. Just as space provides the underlying opportunity to incorporate all of the newest machinery, place provides its realities. Just as a Paradigm Shift provides the opportunity, Paradigm Processing provides its certainty.

# Chapter 11

*Nothing in life will come to past without the process and without process, there is no need for the space.*

We live in a three-dimensional world. The configuration of the space around us molds and directs our actions and interactions. Through our experiences, we become highly skilled at organizing and explaining space for our personal or interactive purposes.

For instance:

- The objects we work with on our jobs are most often arranged closest to us. Computer keyboards, current documents, common reference materials, and favorite pieces of music might immediately surround us in an office, while other materials are kept further away in filing cabinets, or desk drawers. Just as the mental images we have most often are generally closest to our consciousness and awareness, while we forget the images, actions, or interactions related to something considered un-important or unpleasing.

- Physical space is structured according to uses and inter-actions. An office door can be closed to give a feeling of independence from the space outside, or left open to welcome others in. Your office is more likely to be near a colleague's office – just as our mental state or memory is constructed according to uses and needs for interaction. We forget and close our minds to those experiences that do not affect us personally, and open our minds and retain those things that bring us happiness (e.g., we think about our children, spouses, and family because it is closest to our heart, mind, and consciousness).

The young man I had an altercation with and talked about earlier in the previous chapter is reliving the fight we had, and it is still being replayed in his memory because it is still close and a clear part of his awareness. I believe to this day, he is still carrying that experience around with him, guiding, and influencing him. Now, I also remember being in a fight that I lost that same year. I was beaten really badly. My eyes were swollen shut, my lips and jaw had been hit so many times and had puffed-up to the point that some people did not recognize me. Although, I was beaten that day, I went to school the next day to see him walking through the halls. I had to go to school everyday with the person that beat me up and I lived through it. As-a-matter-of-fact, if I saw him today, I would not recognize him. The young man I fought and talked about earlier in the previous chapter did not attend my school and never had to see me again. Nonetheless, it still had a profound effect on him as if it had happened yesterday.

The point is, at that time, space, and place the young man from the fight and I had the same experience, we both lost a fight, and remembered the beating vividly. We had let those events become a part of us at that time, in that space and place, a part of our awareness. If he had not run from me at the university, I think I could have helped him through the processes at the university, but by running, he closed himself off to the possibility of developing a relationship, and the

**63**

opportunity to receive the gift of discourse, of help, that I had to offer him.

"People who let events and circumstances dictate their lives are living reactively. That means that they do not act on life they only react to it." (Graham, 1997)

Practice: Are you letting negative events and circumstances dictate your life? If so, what are they?

Share your thoughts here:

_____

_____

_____

_____

_____

_____

Reflecting on these events helps us in the healing process, and it encourages us to relive and continue those events that were positive in our lives.

# Chapter 12

*Reactive people do not take responsibility for their own lives and their own feelings. They feel good about themselves only if other people say nice things to them, or criticize them; they let it affect their view of themselves (Graham, 1997).*

Fear comes in many forms, as it affects our relationships, our actions and reactions, which affect future blessings or gifts. Although fear is an emotion crucial to survival, fear also has a negative effect on what others believe about us, and the motivation behind any action or transactions. Nonetheless, in order to achieve an all-around positive effect in our relationships and transactions, the goals that we have – have to be all-inclusive and all positive. For example, relationships have multiple dimensions, which connect negatively or positively within time.

If you have ever taken an algebra course, you know that if you multiply a negative number by a negative number the answer would always be a positive number. Alternatively, in Paradigm Processing negative actions multiplied by negative actions equal positive outcomes and reactions. The idea is that your actions and reactions create an effect on others' perceptions of you. However positive or negative, it has a short and long-term effect on future endeavors. You are creating an outcome where everyone in that culture or in your presence wins even if two or more negative actions are present.

For instance a friend of mine, who graduated from the same university as I, went on to open his own company. He had an employee, at the company that he had just started, that was not doing their job, costing monetary, and employee losses. He stated that this person was slowly discrediting his reputation as the leader of the company he started. At the same time, the employee was decreasing their work output, and increasing negative gossip, thus, making the working environment miserable for everyone. This person had been testing his character, his leadership ability(s) and had been doing it publicly for a little over six months. The bad thing about that situation was that that person was his sister who was a single parent of four children. He had extensive discussions with her about her behavior. She couldn't explain herself. His hands were tied because she was family. He asked himself, "What do I do? Do I fire her? If she worked for someone else, would they have fired her?"

He decided not to fire her. However, he did decrease her hours from full-time to part-time, and informed her that if her behavior continued she would be fired. I asked him, "How did that help the work environment? How did that help your sister? And, how did it help you?" He stated, "Because, I took a stand with my sister, her actions changed, thereby causing a change among the other employees. Their work output increased, people started coming to work on time or early, and there were more smiles, jokes, and laughter within the various departments, which made it a pleasure to come to work." He stated, "My sister changed how and what she said to people, how she was perceived as an employee, and she eventually became a trainer." Incidentally, his sister eventually quit and found other employment that paid her more money. He stated that she had been working there for a year and a half without incident.

My friend made it clear that he valued the work environment, he valued his sister, he wanted his employees to feel good about their jobs, and that he valued their contributions to the company. He went on to say, "My sister actually helped me to become a better leader." I asked "How?" and he said, "Although the way she did it was wrong, I think she showed me some of my faults as a leader, and she showed me how to increase productivity without hurting anyone."

Understanding your environment is not tricky, because you created your environment knowingly and unknowingly. You created it first in your mind and then in your actions. Manifesting your successful future requires the development of an attitude of worth, and an attitude of deserving the best relationships in the best culture and environment. By doing righteous things, in your actions, and demeanor, sometimes it will bring out truths from those who we may think have negative intentions, as well as positive ones. However, those same individuals who include negative discourse in their dialog may be conduits for bringing out the best in us, thus making better people in our current environment. We previously talked about a negative number "multiplied" by a negative number equaling a positive number. Well, positive discourse (+pd) "multiplied" by positive discourse (+pd) also equals a positive outcome (+o) where everyone wins (+pd x +pd = +o).

In other words, everyone that meets you or has discourse with someone about you walk away with a positive feeling and optimism about you. People benefit from your endeavors and actions on all occasions, whether the discourse is all positive or all negative – the outcome is positive because both actions are consistent. Personal actions that are consistently positive or negative, creates an environment where everyone know their place in that culture or relationship. On-the-other-hand, as with the equation where a negative multiplied by a positive number would equal a negative number, +pd x -pd = -o. The metaphor of the equation is that inconsistent actions, +pd x -pd, equals an inconsistent outcome, -o, damages to relationships and society in whole. Whereas, consistent behavior builds trust and a positive paradigm of who and whom we are, and helps us to achieve our goals.

# Chapter 13

*Good leaders who lead with courage and conviction are consistently positive. However, inconsistent leaders build mistrust, a distrustful environment; thus slowing down human mental capital, and productivity.*

Courage Conviction Leadership (CCL) is an ideology of what people envision for themselves and how that vision is seen and retained by others. For example, higher education lecturers and theorist have always recognized the enormous gap that exists between leadership approaches and practical working applications in today's complex educational and business systems. It is my belief that as we live by courage, conviction, and self-leadership we enable ourselves to live longer, healthier, and economically secure. We can do this by sharpening those leadership skills through practical suggestions and information identified in this book. If you follow the simple rules addressed, it will enable individuals to improve their personal relationships with courage and conviction. It is all about not being fearful of the truth. The truth improves relationships with colleagues, subordinates, students, and community leaders by inducing greater energy surges in every aspect of your life. Some of the characteristics and values of a leader with courage and conviction are:

1. Most people believe that their talents are distributed normally and none of us are really as good as he or she would like to think, however, a leader would find a way to help you find what you are good at and enjoy doing. The Courage Conviction Leader believes that by focusing on what you are good at, he or she creates a situation that would be considered a "win-win" because you would   become successful doing what you love to do and the leader would feel successful by helping you do it.

2. Our imaginative, symbolic right brain is at least as important as our rational, deductive left. We reason by faith at least as often as with good data. "Does it feel right?" counts for more than "Does it add up?" or "Can I prove it?" The Courage Conviction Leader cares less about your feelings than the data; it is the mutual understanding, the reciprocal learning, and then you and I can win in the end.

3. Courage Conviction Leaders believe that we are creatures of our environment, very sensitive and responsive to external rewards and punishment. We are also strongly driven from within or self-motivated when we think others have our best interest at heart.

4. Courage Conviction Leaders express beliefs with a harsh honesty where actions speak louder than words. They watch for patterns and are wise enough to distrust words that in any way conflicts with our deeds. In other words, if you do not have a talent or gift in the area you are working in, he or she would say, "Maybe you should try another area, something that brings you happiness."

The Courage Conviction Leader desperately believes that everyone should have meaning in his or her lives. [Individuals] simultaneously need their independence, and need to live fully in their independence, with the abilities that they were called or blessed to do (Peters, & Waterman Jr., 1982).

**(Read Aloud)**
**I will have the courage to lead with conviction.**

Courage Conviction Leadership (CCL) and Paradigm Processing will, for those who witness it consciously or unconsciously whether in business or education, lead to self-motivated higher output and smoother operations in their lives. It establishes a balance between what we value, and how and why we work at keeping it. Having courage and conviction is all about how being honest in leadership guarantees happiness. It's all about avoiding the pitfalls of being too lenient or too domineering in relationships.

The main point is producing a closer match between the knowledge of who we are, where we are, how we relate, and why we react to certain situations. The CCL model is a tool to enhance morale through leadership and encourages information as a means to a proactive end of any situation. The way in which we see or envision our life should shape our decision-making. Conversely, the way we see what is presented to us via communication and information determines what we are to do in life.

This leadership style is that ability to lead with convictions for the good of the business, self, community, society, and etc. It is having the ability to analyze the situation from a psychological, analytical, and spiritual perspective. For some, the decision might be a shock and may hurt initially, but in the end, the decision had been made from defining research. In this context, it is the ability to make a decision for the benefit of all. Courage Conviction Leadership is a combination of Authoritarian, and Servant Leadership (leaders that want to serve).

Courage Conviction Leadership (CCL) is about living life to its fullest, concentrating more on pragmatism or common sense in decision-making. I recognize that learning takes place in a wide variety of different contexts – economic, social, and cultural areas (Haddad, 1996). Throughout life we all go through some adversity, at that time, space, and place of hardship, it takes a great deal of courage to use common sense rather than a uniform prescription to life.

For example, often men and women have unprotected sexual intercourse. It takes courage to think in terms of not accepting the opportunity to have sexual intercourse, and even more courage to say "no" to the invitation. The decision to be a leader – to take ownership for what happens in your life is having the conviction to know the difference between right and wrong and loving yourself enough to know and understand the consequences of your actions. In today's society, our interactions with one another have to be evaluated in terms of questioning, self-reflection, criticism, and recommendations. Having the courage to de-emphasize differences and emphasize those methods of connecting healthy and/or unhealthy realities will enhance our ability to live a long life of joy.

**(Read Aloud)**
**For my health and for the health of the people I love, I will have the courage to tell the truth about a negative situation.**

Interconnected relationships and truthful, honest participation is clearly an act of love. As I stated earlier, understanding self-limitations and abilities through Courage Conviction Leadership helps each individual in society not just the ones we love, but everyone; Like the members of a band, the music is only as good as the notes being played, the connection between each member of the band, and the collective needs of the musician's individuality. People only gain prestige and fulfillment by harmonizing with the people they connect with in terms of making everyone better off because of the connection.

Understanding self-reflection and connections to each other's collective needs motivate human behavior, which is seldom simple. Leadership philosophy is effective only so long as they function as such, for and with the collective. When human beings begin to suffer from lack of honesty, their functions are naturally impaired. In other words, we are all leaders of our actions and thoughts, and when we allow ourselves to succumb to things that are detrimental to our joy, to our success, and happiness in life, we must reflect individually about how we react as leaders. When individuals and national leaders cease to perform their functions honestly, the society itself is seriously weakened. It is important, therefore, to understand the factors that keep groups together, that interconnectedness that we all share.

**(Read Aloud)**
**I will not be discouraged or deviate from my goals of achieving holistic wealth. I will have encouraging thoughts, discourse, and actions in my life.**

Most people, over-time, have a tendency to deviate or depart from the expected practices that initially formed the basis of relationships, such as, discouraging discourse, i.e., the discourager. Those discouraging actions can make or break the connections within relationships that initially brought joy. The discourager is a person who is constantly diverging sharply from encouraging, or displaying such divergent discouraging behavior that it affects the physical world (Encarta, 2009). The discourager violates the rights of other members connected to him or her. The discourager fails to follow the norms set forth – written, socially, implicitly and explicitly. The discourager is a person who does not have the courage to honestly and truthfully lead with encouraging foresight, but with discouraging insight. His or her actions challenge your faith, joy, your possibilities, your ideas, and your very existence. These people have to be dealt with truthfully and honestly or your relationships will begin to implode.

Being a discourager is something found in behavior, it reflects influenced behavior and has to be checked constantly in our physical actions. In regards to the CCL model, being encouraging or discouraging is an individual matter as it is a social matter. However, once discouragement is uncovered, the outcome is a leadership practice. A practice that means that, out of love, you might have to fire someone you love. You might lose a friend, but gain social and self-respect, and eventually the love and respect will return. It involves respecting values and norms, which are not universal among individuals. For example, if you are about to have unprotected sex without asking if the other person has been tested for a sexual disease, you are not acting in accordance with the CCL model. The CCL model encourages individuals to have the courage and conviction to ask the question, "Have you been tested?" and to follow through for Paradigm Processing, self-actualization and preservation. For the good of the paradigm and the social order, understanding the discourager, indeed, is such a complex and important aspect of leadership in social behavior in a society as a whole (Greenleaf, 1997).

**(Read Aloud)**
**I will organize and eliminate the clutter in my life everyday so that it will lead to my life in victory and joy.**

A further stage in the dynamics of the model is disorganization. So far, we have primarily been concerned with the forces that bring people together, and keep them together by having the courage to react effectively to situations. However, we also need to discuss the decision to sacrifice our time and our dedication. A lack of self-sacrifice in leadership can cause disorganization and instability within the philosophy and more importantly our relationships. The perception of self-sacrifice is a large motivating force when people need to see their leader go that extra mile. Seeing the leader go that extra mile can reverse any negative process, in effect, keeping people together psychologically and socially.

In the philosophy of disorganization there are at a minimum three psychological factors that present itself:

- **First, the needs of the individual would be satisfied without recourse;**
- **Second, the needs of the individual are still there, and**
- **Third the belief that individual needs cannot be satisfied (Rathus, 1993).**

The latter two are very significant to disorganization, because members no longer believe in the leader and their ability to capably act with courage and conviction. It is in-effect a function of business relationships, and a precursor for personal relationships. In other words, if the needs continue to exist in relationships, sabotage and disorganization is the result.

In the CCL model, social relationships are the central factors in the leadership process. The process should be a reciprocal process where each individual is treated fairly and each individual's needs are being met with conviction and honesty. It is also about acting responsibly with one another. The methodology is merely a symbolic or representational process for those individuals who have been embedded in a society of selfishness for a long time. The CCL model goes against the social ideology that someone has to win and that someone has to lose. In that type of organization or relationship, selfish personal needs are being met at the expense of others. It can get so bad that encouraged people can become discouraged thus becoming a co-dependent in the relationship.

**(Read Aloud)**
**I will have the courage to develop "win/win" outcomes in all facets of my life.**

CCL is a scientific approach to the process and takes place in social settings. Human beings are social animals that engage in reciprocal patterns of expectations that are constantly forming, solidifying, weakening, shifting, or breaking up. In these social interactions and dynamic processes, the organization or relationship is in a constant state of unstable equilibrium. The CCL model leaves very little room for instability because it rules with truthfulness, information gained from research, and honesty for the good of the paradigm and the whole. The CCL model starts with information and the best decision alternative.

Suppose you see or hear someone taking on the role of the discourager in a relationship or in your organization. You want to confront that individual, and you are looking for the best possible situational outcome or "win/win" decision: $d_1$, $d_2$,. For example, I remember an assistant manager telling me about the leadership style of the manager of the store where he worked. He stated that the manager believed in letting the organization run itself, a laissez-faire governing style. He went on to state that it was frustrating because of the number of discouragers, selfish, and self-regulating individuals working there. He could not get any work done. He decided to call the district manager. However, when he called, the district manager was not there, and the only person he could talk to was the secretary, whom he considered a friend. He told the secretary everything that was on his mind.

He became a discourager and could not control the negative things that came out of his mouth. Needless-to-say, the secretary did not talk to the district manager about the situation, but she did talk to the manager of the store where he worked, which created additional problems for the assistant manager. Now, the secretary did not know that the assistant manager had already talked to the manager who stated that he should try to fit into the culture.  As a result, three things occurred:

- **Loss of the secretary's friendship**
- **Loss of the manager's trust, and**
- **Loss of an opportunity to create a paradigm as an encourager.**

Figure 6 shows the best possible outcome for the assistant manager had he used the CCL model; the positive response to your conviction under each of the two possible conditions within the state of nature (High Acceptance $s_1$, and $s_2$,). The State of Nature is a term used in social interactions to describe a condition of compassion. There are some sociologist and philosophers who believe that the State of Nature is uncompassionate and the opposite occurs (Stuckenberg, 1888).

In the latter situation, we will make a decision scientifically based on information, research, and time. The outcome would be a favorable or unfavorable decision to inform the district manager. We will use the research indicator of $I_1$, or $I_2$; then a decision $d_1$, $d_2$, or $d_3$ will be made; finally, the State of Nature $s_1$, or $s_2$, will occur. State of Nature is used here in terms of a social practice to describe the theoretical condition between the manager and assistant manager before the legitimate use of physical force, or a discussion with the district manager. The decision and the State of Nature combine to provide a final "win/win" outcome for all involved. The probabilities of occurrence are (P).

The first piece to the model is research, see Figure 6:

**FIGURE 6**

| | Research Report | |
|---|---|---|
| State of Nature | Favorable $I_1$, | Unfavorable $I_2$, |
| High Acceptance, $s_1$ | $P(I_1 \mid s_1) = .90$ | $P(I_2 \mid s_1) = .10$ |
| High Acceptance, $s_2$ | $P(I_1 \mid s_2) = .25$ | $P(I_2 \mid s_2) = .75$ |

Note that these probability estimates provide a reasonable degree of confidence in the information. If the true State of Nature is $s_1$, the probability of favorable information regarding any outcome ($I_1$) is .90 and the probability of unfavorable information regarding the possible outcome is ($I_2$) or .10. If the true State of Nature is $s_2$, the probability of a favorable outcome is .25 and the probability of an unfavorable outcome is .75. The reason for the .25 probability of potentially misleading information on the characteristics of the individuals involved. Figure 7, illustrates how time affects the relationship whether there was perfect information, perfect information about the State of Nature, or without perfect information.

**FIGURE 7: Courage Conviction Leadership Model**
**(Constant Changes)**

| DATA | New Information to the Individual | Beginning Stages of Understanding | Complete Understanding | Decline in Knowledge |
|------|------|------|------|------|
| | $S_1$ | $S_2$ | $S_3$ | $S_4$ |
| | | | | |
| TIME | | | | |

Figure 7 shows that over-time the information, whether accepted or rejected will begin a new way of thinking for the assistant manager. The slope declines and starts again with new information on the subject because of time. Figure 8 shows the different stages of dealing with the situation over-time with more data/information – the conviction to follow-up, an understanding of how it contributes to relationships and social order, advice giving with courage and conviction, and finally, self-directed in actions as a leader, accepting and believing that everyone can have a "win/win" outcome (Covey, 1989).

**FIGURE 8**

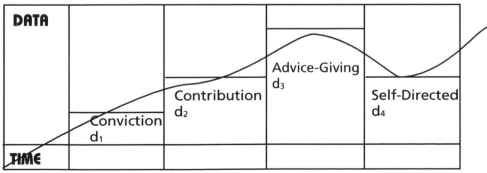

Legend:
*Data: Flow of information for decision-making*
*Time: Reflection and time to maturity*

Courage Conviction Leadership is a leadership methodology, shown in Figures 6-8, which restrains the worse in people. It is about researching the truth, understanding how new knowledge is produced over time, and how we should respond to create a "win/win" outcome. The leader acknowledges a basic fact from the data and reacts, proactively, with an authoritarian hand that leaves little room for doubt in the outcome. CCL has outcomes that are psychologically, sociologically, economically, and politically best for all involved in that particular environment. Note: the action may not be taken with the agreement of all involved because, sometimes you might have to go to the district manager or go over someone's head to get positive results (Bittel, 1984).

Finally, as I previously stated, the manager of the store confronted the assistant manager about fitting into the culture, but he also thought that the assistant manager was trying to take his job, and that he was envious of the manager. I told him that he needed to understand that by seeking out the support of the district manager, it looked like he was envious and wanted the manager's job.

**(Read Aloud)**
**I will chase my dreams, envying no one, by putting in my time.**

Another personal fact that may be holding people back from reaching their full potential is envy. Envy is a product of fear. You cannot focus on what others are doing. If you occupy yourself with what others are doing you will never accomplish any goals. If the accomplishments of others consume you to the point where it distracts you or makes you angry, this will cause a delay in your dreams. You must first recognize that you are envious and then you must turn that envy into a knowledge building experience. An experience that leads beyond what you envy. By doing that, you change envy and fear into something to learn from, something gained, and most importantly, something that will help you to grow.

**(Read Aloud)**
**I will predetermine my mind to succeed.**

We all know that negativity exists and that we have no control over its appearance regardless of any beliefs or ideology we try to maintain. However, we do have control over our response to its appearance and control over its outcome, which should always result in a "win/win" ending. Your "win/win" attitude and positive visions will change what people see in you, and what they think about you. I think the biggest lesson that anyone can learn is the stupendous importance of what we think. If I knew what you thought, I would know who you are, for your thoughts predetermine who you are. By changing our thoughts, we can change our lives.

You must set your thoughts and perceptions on the goal of increased confidence, increased wealth, increased faith, and most importantly, your physical and emotional discourse. From now on, you must think positively to predetermine your success in all endeavors. In order for this to happen, you must develop an upbeat outlook. You must have an outlook and an optimism about the outcome of your efforts to be the best you can be. You must engage in characteristics that predetermine a future of success through determination upon every word and action. You have to be self-assuredly devoted to your ability to achieve your goals.

Here is an example of the need for unyielding fortitude on the part of anyone who wants to meet the challenge of Paradigm Processing their future. The person I am writing about earned his Bachelor's of Arts degree quickly and effectively, leaving a positive impression on everyone. However, the first time he stood up to speak in college, words failed him. He could not get beyond the middle of the five-minute presentation that his professor had assigned. As he stood in front of his class, ready to give his presentation, his face went white, and he hurried off the platform in tears.

The fundamental issue for him was that he would graduate early if he could only rid himself of the fear and complete the task of public speaking to pass that final speech course. I told him that he could predetermine his future by changing his mindset, by being fearless, and by motivating himself with the fact that he would be graduating from a quality university. He used some positive experiences to motivate himself to complete the presentation. He thought of all of the people he was earning his degree for, and all of the people who had come before him to make this experience possible. He completed the task successfully, got a good grade, and graduated.

**(Read Aloud)**
**I will create a system that predetermines my success.**

Creating a Predetermined System of Success in any environment or setting starts with the understanding that everyone has abilities above, beyond, and underneath what you initially see. Recognizing that is important to accomplishing your goals of creating successful relationships, becoming an educated researcher, and developing a faithful philosophy that leads to holistic wealth. The system is about what we have been discussing, and that is Paradigm Processing, building, and maintaining positive relationships through discourse and actions.

**(Read Aloud)**
**I will build and maintain positive relationships.**

First, be sure to recognize the contributions of the people you know by recognizing him or her in front of their peers; from the brilliant researcher to the perpetual artist. That public recognition will do wonders for making him or her feel like a winner, and a proud member of that society and in that relationship.

Second, make sure that you provide personal attention to each relationship, work on each relationship individually, measure the strength of the relationship, and privately analyze the growth. If there has been some stagnation, try to understand why, and then try to encourage growth. When you treat each relationship with individual attention, people feel more valued.

Third, be sure to treat every relationship with respect. That should be understood, but sometimes even the simplest ideas need a gentle reminder. Even though, you may feel that some people do not deserve your respect, the trick is - is that that relationship is just as important as the obvious relationship where respect has been earned. People are always watching, trying to earn respect from one another. They will respect the fact that your response to obvious negativity is consistently positive, which creates an environment that maintains and invites winning relationships.

Finally, be consistent. Special treatment can quickly breed resentment among the ranks in relationship building and maintenance. By holding everyone to the same rules and standards, you will set the tone that all of your relationships contribute to all of the success stories in your life. Overall, remember to pay attention to each relationship. Create a system that circumnavigates failure and predetermines success. This is simply making everyone in your environment feel like a championship player in your life.

**(Read Aloud)**
**I will build-up and maintain my success community.**

Successful relationships turn into successful communities. Like those communities, where things get done for the betterment of the society, are built on the efforts of good relationships, solid producers and a few overachievers. Again, to maintain consistent relationships be sure not to spend more time with the overachievers than you would with the producers. When you spend all of your energy only recognizing the overachievers, you alienate the backbone of your success. For example, if you had a car with new tires, custom interior and exterior, but an engine that leaks transmission fluid and oil, how strong or durable would the foundation of that car be? The foundation and underpinning of that car would eventually breakdown and become inoperable. Alternatively, when you ignore the foundation and groundwork of your relationships, they erode over-time, and before you know it, your success crumbles.

Even if they are valuable members of your relationship community, if you ignore people constantly they will feel like losers. When they feel like losers, two things will happen. First, they will start performing like losers. Their performance will head south, and your valuable secondary relationships will soon dissolve. Second, they will start to feel disconnected and unworthy, and when that happens, priceless relationships will erode.

How do you avoid that erosion in your relationship community? You need to create a relationship community where everyone in that community feels like a winner. It may sound kind of unconventional, but appreciation and recognition are two of the most important factors in motivating and maintaining relationships.

## (Read Aloud)
## Speak up!

You can control your paradigm by working on your strength of mind, by making a list of personal goals and objectives you want to achieve through relationship and community building. Opportunities to have discourse about your goals and objectives are on all sides of the universal spectrum and should be exercised whenever possible. Join organizations and volunteer for offices that will require you to talk about your goals and encourages others to get involved. Stand up and assert yourself to enhance your abilities. Do not take a backseat to anyone when it comes to your abilities, they only get better when you exercise and value your capabilities.

Speak up! Join any group where you will have an opportunity to participate actively in the meetings and allows you to have discourse that connects the group to your goals. You have but to look around to see that there is scarcely a single business, community, political office, professional, or even neighborhood activity that does not challenge you to step forward and speak up about your abilities, your goals, and your vision. You will never know what progress you can make unless you have true faith, work hard, and speak your abilities into existence.

People who have discourse about their visions and experiences resulting from what they foresee have taught themselves to remain focused on their goals. I know from experience as a motivational speaker and educator that listeners are easily persuaded to accept your vision if you use personal experiences, and other past successes. They would rather hear about you soaring into the realms of success and happiness, where fortunately the air is not unpretentious for ordinary mortals to breathe. In other words, they can reach the sky just like you.

Those individuals who attend my seminars, or take my courses often give editorials, which is good because I am always hungry for information from successful visionaries. Paradigm Processing is very much an effort to listen to editorials, especially an individual who has earned the right to editorialize. The point is this, create discourse about what life has taught you and I will be your devoted listener, as long as it relates to me or those who can benefit from being around me. Make me feel your experiences are worthy of my attention and your experiences will become my actions.

**(Read Aloud)**
**I will do self-examination for self-renewal each and every day.**

By self-examining your inner most motivations and feelings, you come to terms with them and move on to the future. Additionally, by understanding what influences your motivations, feelings, and behavior, whether proactive or reactive, you can change. You can change those things you do not need and keep those you do need. In addition, you can create a vision for your life that focuses on your potential and the possibilities rather than on your past and the limitations that you have had. In the self-renewal process, think about a desirable "proactive outcome" at the onset and on every level. For example, even when we are discussing the highly volatile subject of the first African-American President with a most openly racist individual – we can still come away with an agreement to disagree. Other subjects that ignite dialog are discussions about religion or politics.

Because, you and I know what subjects starts an argument, the question then becomes:

- **Is it not evident that some people start arguments during discourse for the sole purpose of exchanging ideas?**

- **When we have discourse, do we have a need to arouse creative tension that provokes proactive reactions?**

- **Is it wise to start by saying, "I am going to prove so and so?" Aren't the people you are having discourse with going to accept that as a test of their will, a test of their character, and think to him or herself, "Let's see you do it?"**

- **Isn't it more advantageous to begin by stressing something that you and all of the participants believe, and then raise some pertinent questions that everyone would like to have answered, or agree with?**

Now, take the questions on a heartfelt search for resources, actions, and answers. While on that search, present the facts as you see them so clearly that people will see negative discourse as a method of achieving a positive conclusion.

# Chapter 14

*Those who can personalize their argument can legitimize their explanation with genuineness.*

In every controversial situation where there is an opportunity to be reactive or proactive there is something to be learned or gained. No matter how wide and bitter the differences, there is always some common ground of agreement on which the discourse is legitimized from experiences, not assumptions; discourse where you invite everyone to meet with uprightness and certainty.

To illustrate, there is the story of Debra Jackson, manager of Student Internship of New Ventures, who received a call from her boss on the weekend informing her of an opportunity for a new ten thousand dollar contract; which must be submitted by Thursday. Ms. Jackson sends a group email to her university's student interns for an emergency meeting on Monday at 7:00 a.m. At the meeting, Debra selects Kelvin Spencer a senior at the university to play a key role. He fails to check his email on Sunday because of a family outing and misses the 7:00 a.m. meeting.

The next morning, Debra informs Kelvin of the key role she has for him to play – that it would guarantee him a job that would pay him $75K a year. However, it does involve a high level of travel and she needs an answer immediately. When Kelvin excitedly shares this opportunity with his pregnant wife, Gloria, she expresses concern about the other classes needed to graduate, the travel involved, greater domestic responsibilities for their future child and compromise of her own educational and career aspirations. Nevertheless, she agrees to leave the decision up to him.

Given Kelvin's competence and potential, it is Debra's responsibility to assist/coach Kelvin in achieving an arrangement that compatibly reconciles his personal, educational and workplace values.

Ultimately, it is still Kelvin's responsibility to make a decision – along with any future probable consequences.

Taking responsibility for your life in this situation means consciously:

1. Discovering what's most important to you – based upon the paradigm you are creating for yourself.
2. Reconciling short-term priniciples of educational and professional aspirations with long-term principles of self, education, family, and service.
3. Deciding the acceptability of your probable future paradigm.
4. Designing and implementing a plan based upon your priniciples.

**(Answer the following questions)**

If you were Kelvin, would you accept the opportunity, given Gloria's concerns? Yes _____ No_____Why?

_____

_____

_____

_____

_____

_____

_____

_____

_____

_____

Alternate Question: If you were Gloria, would you be willing to set aside your education and career aspirations to support Kelvin's opportunity? Yes _____ No_____Why?

_____

_____

_____

_____

_____

_____

_____

_____

_____

Possible consequences may include:
- **Extensive travel**
- **Working overtime**
- **Working at home**
- **Focus on work at the expense of the family**
- **Excessive time away from home**
- **Neglecting one's personal well-being**

This is a decision that would involve consideration of career, education, and family. What are your short-term principles?
- **Fast track professional progression paradigm**
- **Name recognition**
- **Personal wealth**
- **Status**
- **Etcetera**

What are your long-term values?
- **Strong proactive relationships**
- **Health**
- **Faithfulness**
- **Etcetera**

What are your educational and personal-life principles?

_____

_____

_____

_____

_____

_____

_____

_____

_____

What educational and personal-life principles does your answer from Question 1 reflect?

_____

_____

_____

_____

_____

_____

_____

Do you presently live consistent with this (these) principle(s)? Yes ___ No___Why?

_____

_____

_____

_____

_____

_____

_____

This decision will probably have both a short-term and long-term impact on Kelvin's educational and personal life - <u>it is a defining moment!</u>

The best resolution is based upon reconciling educational aspirations and personal desires through principle clarification.

Kelvin informs Debra that he is excited about the career advancement opportunity and would really like to accept the position, but is unsure because of his wife's concerns. When Debra does not get an answer by the end of the workday Tuesday, she chooses someone else. Kelvin experiences frustration and anger about losing this career opportunity.

Is Kelvin 100% responsible and 100% accountable for losing this career advancement opportunity? Yes___ No___Why?

_____

_____

_____

_____

_____

_____

_____

_____

_____

_____

_____

Guidlines for creating a paradigm that is proactive:

1. Support the whole person – by recognizing that personal principles, career and educational responsibilities are inseparable.
2. Support implementation of a student's work-life plan – by clarifying personal principles, educational priorities and responsibilities, and reconciling personal goals with life's necessities.
3. Explore and become knowledgeable of the career aspiration of your direct relationships.

No matter how determined one is to be successful in life, a personal decision that includes others would require a need to convince them to be more proactive than reactive. Debra, the manager was reactive and not proactive to the needs of Kevin and his family. Debra should have set-out immediately to discover a common ground with Kevin. Without that support from Debra, Kevin was left to make a decision that would either hurt himself or his loved ones.

Sometimes we fail to realize that it is people and relationships that will advance our cause to holistic wealth, and business and careers will always advance if they are strong and genuine.

**(Read Aloud)**
**I will surround myself with successful relationships and positive discourse.**

Surrounding him or herself with successful people requires a complete understanding of how discourse works. When we are deepening our relationships, we want to have meaningful discourse. Discourse that may take a little longer because we want to really listen, really inform, be informed, convince, and/or persuade. For example, perhaps you are a university admissions recruiter, adviser, or program chairperson of a civic organization or a member of a women's club and you are faced with the task of informing, entertaining, convincing, recruiting, or persuading a group of people for the first time. The key is that you should not worry about what you are going to say, just relax and go into the discourse with a positive frame of mind.

When going into the discourse with a positive frame of mind, you must not prepare for rejection or for victory; just a simple dialog with others. Preparation for rejection or victory is not always a good thing because it actually helps to bring about one or the other, a loss or a victory. That is not good because that means that one person would come out on top of the other, which means the possible loss of a relationship that could have been more productive in the future. No, just let the inspiration come to you, think on your feet and in most occasions it will not fail, and you will remain proactive and positive.

Your discourse serves the same purpose as a verbal social introduction to everyone in the listening vicinity. It brings you, your relationships, and the audience together, establishes a community atmosphere, and creates a bond of interest between relationships. The man who says, "You don't have to be positive and proactive all the time, all you have to do is gain experience, and get more education," is guilty of derailing your career, your relationships, and your standing in the community. Positive discourse starts now, with the next person you talk to, and every other person after that. No relationship or career is more mangled than with the people who have discourse that leaves one person, just one person feeling unimportant.

Discourse is always an introduction into the soul, the spirit, and philosophical ideology. The term, introduction, is the formal presentation of one person to another, to an audience, to society, etc. (Webster's, 1977). The excellent introduction adequately creates a road map for individual's purposes that makes them want to hear what you have to say. Your discourse or introduction ought to lead the listeners inside to the implicit and explicit facts – facts that demonstrate your ability to make positive things happen. In other words, discourse is an introduction that ought to sell the person and the topic, whether it is about your community or your career. Furthermore, it should do these things in the briefest amount of time possible.

That is what discourse ought to do. Discourse is always an introduction of self, and if done incorrectly, it is feeble and inexcusably inadequate. It does not have to be. If you have discourse that is proactive, builds community, builds relationships, and revitalizes the energy of listeners, you are creating a paradigm of yourself that people want to be involved with, and want to be around.

**(Read Aloud)**
**I will control my emotions and behavior when having discourse.**

Make a list of the ways in which you can monitor and manage your emotions and eliminate self-destructive or nonproductive feelings. Write a description of the type of person you want to become: What characteristics do you want to have that you do not have now? What do you admire in others that you do not see in yourself? Suppose you are talking to a few friends about the police officer who stopped you for going one mile over the speed limit. You can tell your friends that story with all of the cool objectivity of a spectator, but it happened to you and you had certain feelings and emotions, which you expressed in quite definite language. "That clown this and that clown that." Additionally, never use the third-person approach because it will not make much of an impression on your old friends or new acquaintances. They want to know exactly how you personally felt when that police officer wrote out that ticket. Therefore, the more you relive the scene you are describing, and re-creating, the more that you put them at the scene, the more vividly they see your vision. The more people can see your vision the more they are gravitated to your side of the incident. You can put them to sleep or you can control their emotions to the point where they want to cry, help, and contribute.

One of the reasons why we go to plays and movies is that we want to hear and see emotions expressed. We have become so fearful of venting our feelings in public that we have to go to a play, church, or watch a movie to satisfy that need for emotional expression. You will generate excitement and interest in proportion to the amount of excitement and emotional expression you put into your discourse. Do not repress your honest feelings; do not put a damper on your authentic enthusiasms. Show your listeners how eager you are to talk about your goals and visions, and you will hold their attention. The key is that you have a goal in mind, which should be proactive toward the needs of everyone involved.

You cannot be successful if you have no vision or if you do not feel worthy of success. Having a vision for your life allows you to live out of hope and faith, rather than out of your reservations. When you have discourse with people, do so with an air of anticipation, not like a man or woman diving into an empty swimming pool. The spring in your walk may be largely put on, but it will do wonders for you and it gives the people who walk into your paradigm a feeling that you have something you are eager and proud to disclose. Just before you begin to intertwine your paradigm with another paradigm, smile for one minute, take a deep breath, and take control of your emotions and behavior. Keep your head high and your chin up. Everytime you open your mouth, you are about to enter another person's paradigm informing them of something worthwhile, and every part of you should inform them of that, clearly and unmistakably. You are in command and you should act as if you are.

This principle of interaction with anyone who is looking and listening is a principle of being proactive in reactive situations, those situations that demand mental awareness, and emotional control. You will be absorbingly interesting because you show a large level of enthusiasm in situations where you have an opportunity to engage people. Above all, remember that these actions of emotional control and behavior will make you feel earnest.

**(Read Aloud)**
**I am confident with infectious passion and earnest enthusiasm.**

You gain confidence by concentrating on your formal and informal education, talents, attributes, and personal history, past failures and successes. Concentrate on all of the things that make you special and unique. You must believe in yourself, in your history and experiences with contagious and earnest enthusiasm. You have to feel worthy of your vision. You have to feel that you deserve success, and you have to feel it with infectious passion.

Contradicting ideas are much less likely to arise in people's mind when your discourse presents ideas that people are passionate about.

Infectious passion is just that – it shoves aside all negative and opposing ideas. When your aim is to produce a life of wealth, faith, and health, remember it is more productive to stir positive emotions than to arouse negative thoughts. Feelings are more powerful than cold ideas.

**(Read Aloud)**
**I will set my goals on a path that creates my joy.**

It does no good to simply have visions unless you surrender yourself to constructing significant actions. You must consider some lifelong actions that will help you realize your dreams. Once you have discovered what brings you joy, the first step is to stakeout that area and stay strictly within those limits. Because, this is what will bring you joy, it will cause you to live a long healthy and enjoyable life. Do not make the mistake of trying to cover all areas.

For example, from my experiences in higher education, most students have majored in two or three subject areas, which caused them to be in school well over the minimum four-year degree requirements. How utterly futile, continually changing your major, not knowing which way to go, not knowing how to enjoy the educational process. The worst scenario was a student that I met in 2002. She had changed her major from nursing, to education, and finally to art. Everytime she changed her major, she received a new advisor, a new curriculum. She had 140 hours out of the 120 minimum needed, and no degree. Now, I do not think that is totally the fault of the student. I think that many of the students, who have changed their major that many times, like this young woman, did not know or was misadvised or not advised at all.

She should have been advised by someone who knew that higher education was an opportunity to find joy, to live a joyful life, and free herself from working in areas that she did not enjoy. In other words, her first major should have been her one and only major. A major or discipline that she had a passion for and was gifted at doing from experience. Moreover, for that reason, most students that go to college or a university barely get beyond their first year before they change their major, or quit altogether.

I would like to say that this was an extreme example. However, I have heard hundreds of students talk about subject areas that failed to hold their attention because they really did not enjoy the subject matter, or that they just were not talented in that area. Another example would be the young man that came into my office telling me how his family really wanted him to be a medical doctor. Yet, the student was barely passing his biology courses, and did not like dissecting a pig, or working around corpses. On the other hand, the student was earning A's in the social sciences. You would think that someone along the way would have told him that he was not gifted or called to be in the medical field, but was gifted and talented in areas where people needed an understanding of Social and Psychological issues. After talking to him, I found that he enjoyed helping people, not helping them medically, but socially, and psychologically. Long story short, he went on to earn his undergraduate degree concentrating in sociology and psychology, and a Masters in Social Work. He is currently working on his Doctorate of Psychology and he is extremely happy about his decision to change his major to one that fit his life goals.

Finally, to set your goals on a path that creates joy you must start by thinking about the end first.

What will be your legacy?

_____

_____

_____

_____

_____

What foundation will your goals be built upon?

_____

_____

_____

_____

_____

What values, beliefs, or principles matter most to you?

_____

_____

_____

_____

_____

Why do you want to achieve your goal?

_____

_____

_____

_____

_____

_____

Will society benefit?

_____

_____

_____

_____

_____

_____

Will those around you benefit?

_____

_____

_____

_____

_____

Is it linked to things you believe in?

_____

_____

_____

_____

_____

_____

How? To find the answers, you must:

- Read and learn as much about that goal as possible.
- Find role models whose vision/goals you could study either up close or from a distance.
- Find one or more coach/mentor willing to give you advice and encouragement.
- Make strategic alliances with other individuals, businesses, consultants, and corporations in order to provide a broad range of services.
- Write a mission statement.
- Build a strong network of contacts tied together through personal relationships.

**(Read Aloud)**
**I will find guides, coaches, and mentors to get me through those difficult times.**

From my experiences, some people think of personal and/or public help as charity. They feel as though general discourse from coaches and mentors is a kind of bloated exchange of ideas, not something they can use. However, underneath all of the bloated exchange is where Reciprocal Learning and Paradigm Processing occur. Sometimes we have to look deep into the dialog to get what we need? It takes time to get to what we need from discourse, but it is worth it once we get to it. Most people want and need straightforward dialog from people who have already traveled the pathway. They need coaches and mentors that are willing to put in the time to help; which there are many of them. You want to talk to a person who really knows and has ideas that were conceived from experience, common sense and dedicated to getting you to the next level in your quest for wealth.

What are the differences between mentoring and coaching? These differences are summarized in Figure 9.

**FIGURE 9:** *Differences between Mentoring and Coaching*

|  | **MENTOR** | **COACH** |
|---|---|---|
| **FOCUS** | Individual | Performance |
| **ROLE** | Facilitator with no agenda | Specific agenda |
| **RELATIONSHIP** | Self-selecting | Comes with the job |
| **SOURCE OF INFLUENCE** | Perceived value | Position |
| **PERSONAL RETURNS** | Affirmation/ learning | Teamwork/ performance |
| **ARENA** | Life | Task related |

You are the focal point of your mentor, while the coach is job-focused and performance oriented. A mentor is like a best friend, but you are free to choose what to accept or refute. A coach directs you to some result, the person may choose how to get there, but the coach is deliberately reviewing and watching the growth for value and competence.

Mentorship is people involved in a two-way mutually beneficial relationship. Mentors will let you learn from your experiences so that you can move forward in your endeavors. Mentors never give you solutions. They ask questions so that the solutions will surface. On the other hand, a coach is a more structured person who sets agendas to reinforce dexterity and activities. If I am your mentor, you probably picked me. If I am your coach, I was hired or asked to be in your life.

Interpersonal dexterity determines the effectiveness for both coaches and mentors. The coach also has an indirect or bona fide level of authority by nature of their position, ultimately they can insist on compliance. Mentorship is a power free relationship based on mutual respect. Your coach's job is to form team harmony, and encourage excellent job performance. Your mentor does not have a job, per se, the relationship is reciprocal. It is a learning process for the mentor, from the feedback and insights of the mentee. The mentor mentee connection is a conduit that supports, helps, and develops personal satisfaction. This is a person that listens, builds confidence, faith, and trust.

Although coaching and mentoring is not the same thing, both have results that can be beneficial to you. The mentor provides advice, shares knowledge and experiences, and teaches using a low pressure, self-discovery approach. Mentors teach using an adult learning versus teacher to student model. They are not only willing to question for self-discovery, but also willing to freely share their own experiences and skills with the mentees. Likewise, a coach's job depends on your success. He or she is concerned with your performance, ability to adapt to change, your vision, direction, and work unit (Starcevich, 1998).

**105**

# Chapter 15

*I will walk by true faith, undeni-
able faith, and blinded faith.*

True faith, undeniable faith and blind faith conquers fear. When a
person is under the influence of blind faith, his or her Paradigm
Shifts and enters the 5th dimension. His or her self-confidence is elevated to a metaphysical level. The 5th dimension (the recognition of
divine will) is the communion with your spiritual self. Once your faith is
elevated to those levels, people will see that those feelings of being in-
complete and the bars that may have kept him or her jailed in fear were
brought down by faithfulness. The heat of his or her negative emotions
has been burned away through faith. Everytime he or she acts sponta-
neously, there is that confidence that everything will be alright because
of faith. They talk instinctively with the faith that what is being said is
well organized and developed in the metaphysical for their good.

I shall never forget a discussion I had with one of my spiritual
mentors at my son's football practice. One evening he read a scripture
from the eleventh chapter of Hebrews. He said, "You have heard about
men of faith, I shall not try to tell you what faith is. There are theolog-
ical professors who could do that much better than I can. I am here to
help you understand how faith works." Then my mentor followed that
with such a simple, heartfelt, and majestic expressive definition of faith.
He said, "Faith is those unseen realities, which are eternal. Believe that
what others may say is impossible – is possible."

My mentor's acts of faith were seen in his works with me and others that took the time to listen. His actions were heartfelt actions, which was effective because it rested upon his genuine spiritual worship, and his own inner strength and external life in victory. His true faith was in his work, his willingness to give back, his willingness to discuss what he believed in and that was his secret. He went on to state that, "Yet, I know that advice like this is not popular, it seems vague. It sounds indefinite. The average person wants foolproof rules, something definite, something he or she can put their hands on, rules as precise as the directions for operating a car. That is what I would like to give you." There are rules when it comes to forms of faith. One is work. You can have faith, but you also must give some effort in faith. Secondly, you should give in faith without expecting something in return. As-a-matter-fact, the whole thought of "giving to receive" says that you do not have faith. Faith is truly about working without knowing the end result. However, many believe that hard work takes all the naturalness, spontaneity, and life out of his or her faithful beliefs. When you set goals, you have to keep them always in mind with hard work, and the faith that the hard work will pay off. It is not that you cannot enjoy other aspects of your life, but those faithful goals always have to be at the forefront.

**(Read Aloud)**
**I will take one step toward my goals, and my faith will take me two more steps forward to achieving them.**

Faith is a belief in the trustworthiness of an idea, person, or thing. Faith does not rest on logical proof or material evidence. When I first spoke in public of the gratification of Paradigm Processing and the 4R Model, I touched upon what I believed (more than any other one factor) contributed to my success. Moreover, my success was completely self-directed with faith, reflections, reciprocal learning, research, and responsibility to the community. I followed the directions that will be discussed in the next chapters. Moreover, I did these things because I wanted to do them, and I envisioned myself as a successful, wealthy, and healthy person. I projected myself into the future and then worked toward bringing that projection into reality. That is exactly what you must do with complete faith.

Concentrate your attention on your faith, self-confidence and the ability to work self-directed and self-motivated. Think of what it may mean to you socially, of the friends it will bring, of your increased capacity to be of service in your civic, social, or church group, and of the influence you will be able to exert in your business. In short, concentrating on faith will prepare you for leadership.

In the history of theology, many men have drawn attention to themselves by faith. Many years ago a young man, who was then pastor of a small church with a congregation of about 20 in the Chicago-land area discussed the faith he had in his ability to complete his undergraduate degree while serving his congregation. We talked about how he wanted to build a new church, and how his congregation was rapidly growing. He came into my office full of hope, but he had never attended a higher education institution. Nevertheless, he registered each semester, spring, summer, and fall, taking a full load of courses. Today he has his undergraduate degree, working on his Master's degree in Divinity, and is the pastor of a church that has a congregation of 3000 people.

**(Read Aloud)**
**I will talk about it, shout about it, walk, swim in it, and make body gestures that indicate that I have true faith in individuals, my abilities, and circumstances.**

There is no predicting how far true faith will take you. Some years back, one of my students in one of my courses, said, "The ability to effectively have discourse through faith with others and win their co-operation is an asset that moves mountains and men to the top." Think of the satisfaction and pleasure that will be yours when you know by faith that when you are able to stand up and confidently do anything that will bring you joy. I have traveled across the United States of America, but I know of few things that give greater delight than holding an audience by the power of the spoken word, and sharing of discourse. You get a sense of strength, a feeling of power when you know that you can a person's life.

Now, imagine yourself living with joy on your job, in your profession, and/or in your business. See yourself stepping forward with true faith and confidence upon your vision. You need to feel yourself with the attentive absorption and passion of faith. Feel the wrath of ecstasy upon the completion of your goals as you encounter your new life. Now, envision yourself hearing the words of appreciation from individuals that you have helped. Finally, see yourself showing your appreciation to those who helped you to achieve your goals, and those you have helped in the process. Believe me, there is a magic in it and a never-to-be-forgotten thrill in knowing that you can achieve anything by faith.

Faith and passion will bring joy, and wealth, and will eliminate stress and depression. In other words, if you care enough for a result, care enough for the people in your life, you will most certainly attain joy in your life. If you have faith in goodness, you will be good. If you have faith in your ability to obtain that degree, you will obtain that degree. Only when you have faith, truly have faith in your joy and vision of life, with exclusiveness, and not wish one hundred other incompatible things just as strongly, you will be successful.

Learning to go for your vision of life effectively brings other benefits than merely the ability to dream. As-a-matter-of-fact, to dream with faith and confidence in your life, the benefits to form those actions will unfold initially. The one thing about faith is that it is the road to assurance. It gives you the assurance that every goal, and vision will open up like a blooming flower. Once you realize that you can obtain your dreams, visions, and goals intelligently, it is logical to assume that you can obtain one goal, go for another goal, obtain it, go for another goal, obtain it, and so on. Many men and women have told me that they took my course or came to my sessions because, first, someone told them about my abilities to motivate and encourage. Second, what they learned will go well beyond a grade or just a good feeling, but something that they would use throughout life. It is always my goal that meeting me and talking to me, would be a defining moment in someone's life.

# Chapter 16

*Pause – Take a minute to think about your journey and then begin in faith.*

When people take my course or attend one of my sessions they learn how to change their future with faith, Paradigm Processing, Courage Conviction Leadership, and the 4R Model. They become aware of the irrationality of negative self-consciousness and fear. After the course is over, our relationship is not over. I would see it in their actions and from their discourse, that they had changed – a Paradigm Shift had occurred. Some talked about how they began to impress others, i.e., their families, friends, business associates, customers, and clients, with their newly found faith and understanding. Many of them stated that because he or she changed their personality, the paradigm of those around them changed.

This type of understanding and training also affects the personality in ways that are not immediately apparent. When I asked one of my students what, in his opinion, were the benefits of understanding your paradigm in terms of mental and physical health, he smiled and said he could best answer that question by saying that no prescription could be written to fill the void that was filled in his life. It must be filled by the person engaged in the Paradigm Shift and if he or she thinks he or she cannot fill it, he or she is wrong.

I have the prescription on my desk. Everytime I read it, I am impressed with it:

*Try your best to develop an ability to let others look into your head and heart. Learn to make your thoughts, your ideas, clear to others, individually, in groups, and in public. You will find, as you improve in your effort to do this, that you, your real self, are making an impression, an impact, on people such as you have never done before.*

You can reap a double benefit from this prescription. Your self-confidence strengthens as you learn to live in faith of others, things, and endeavors. Your whole personality grows in depth and breadth. You will be better off emotionally, and if you are better off emotionally, you are better off physically. Understanding the power of faith in our modern world is for everybody, men, and women, young and elderly. It is a wonderful memory, a sense of faith, to have and no pill ever made can give it to you.

The second guidepost, then, is to picture yourself as successful. Now, truly see it in your mind. See the money stacked in perfect piles as high as your belly button in the middle of a bank room. Picture yourself successfully doing what you were afraid of doing by concentrating on the benefits you will receive through faith. Remember, if you care enough, gifted with it, and have faith in it, you will most certainly attain it.

**(Read Aloud)**
**I will take care to think before dialog, because dialog can start or end relationships.**

You can start and end a relationship with the same dialog. It is important to keep your attention off yourself just before you engage in discourse or dialog with one person or a group of people. Concentrate on what the other person or people are saying. Give them your whole-hearted attention, especially if you do not have a complete understanding of the dialog. Sometimes it is important to just be quiet, listen, and let people think you are stupid, than to open your mouth and prove them right.

**(Read Aloud)**
**I will not feel guilty about saying "no."**

I remember on one occasion when I went to hear a speaker who was, according to the television promotion, giving away free books on how to get free government grants and low interest loans. The corporation that the speaker was working for had put together several books that included grants and low interest loans. The books included information on methods of obtaining, retaining, and maintaining grants effectively.

Later the audience and I found out that although the books were free, the program that helps to understand the process would cost $1,000. Now, we all admire a sales person who can put showmanship into their presentation, who are not afraid to express him or herself, not afraid to use their unique method of using discourse, individualism, and imaginative ways of saying what they have to say to the audience. However, this particular speaker was very good at all of the above. So good that people actually forgot that the book was supposed to be free. Without thinking twice, people began to pull their checkbooks from their pockets and their purses. I am sure that all of the people and representatives there really needed a method of obtaining grants to get their programs of the ground and running, but no one questioned the fact that they were being manipulated.

He started the four-hour presentation talking about how successful he was at writing, receiving, and retaining grants with the support of the corporation that he was representing. He displayed pictures of his pretty wife, his big luxurious home, and cars. He also talked about how he experienced many failures before he utilized the services of the corporation. The speaker had created a sensation throughout his presentation that made people in the audience feel as though they could do what he did; achieve the highest level of success using the books he was peddling. The corporation had prepared an illustration to sale their $1,000 set of books and from the start it was just under the guise of free. By insisting that people come early, it afforded the audience the time to have discourse about each of their needs, goals, and the opportunity to receive free information and help. In addition, they made it clear that this program was only offered one time a year and it was a one-time only opportunity. It was obvious that the speaker/salesperson knew that it is not so much as what you say but how you say it.

Nonetheless, in the final portion of his presentation he made his big pitch to sell the books in the back of the room. It was amazing to see half of the room line-up to purchase the book for $1,000 from the discourse of this one person. Although I wanted the book, I decided that I was not going to pay for it. I said, "NO." I said aloud that I was going to get those books at no charge. I said it to my wife, to the person sitting next me, and anyone else who would listen.

I began to talk to everyone that I encountered about the books and the opportunity that it would afford a non-profit organization. About one week after the presentation, I was talking to one of my investment friends about the books, and you know what he said next? He said, "I have those books and you can have them because I do not use them." I said "no" to buying the books and "yes" to the idea that I could obtain them free of charge through discourse and past Paradigm Processing.

The point is if you speak something loudly, and proudly, believe it with true faith – it will come into reality. If you desire it with such intensified naturalness, and let people know what you want, and where you stand, you will draw those people and physical things to you, which can help you to get what you need and want out of life. For this to happen, you must make every window a window of opportunity with positive discourse and actions. Through this Paradigm Process, your magnetism toward positive things will grow stronger and stronger.

**(Read Aloud)**
**To better my knowledge about the area that brings me joy, I will first get the facts about my vision and goals.**

Just like many of you, throughout my life I have had to complete one goal before I went on to another goal. Whether it was starting a business, investing, going to school, or finding my soul mate, I have always started that vision and goal by doing my research in that area. The first thing I did was to put my vision into the space, time, and place that I was currently in. I did it with discourse with others to make my goals and vision of joy real. Having discourse with everyone that came in contact with me, I believe, allowed the space – time to gravitate those individuals and things to me; those individuals and things that could help me to achieve my goals while helping others to achieve theirs.

For example, a man came into my office to discuss the possibility of him attending the university. He really wanted to get his life back on track after losing all of his money. I asked him, "How much money did you lose?" He said, "I lost just fewer than one million dollars." I asked him another question. I said, "If you do not mind telling me, how did you make close to a million dollars?" Now, you must remember this person and others like him came into my office just after I changed my vision. In other words, I drew him or her to me by putting my visions of wealth in the space-time that I was currently in. He went on to tell me that he started his first business when he was in his early 20s. Because he did not have a mentor or coach, he stated, "I failed with the first couple of properties, but I loved what I was doing." He said that he decided to read books and articles about investing in real estate, rent-

**115**

ing, and "flipping" properties. He also stated that he had discourse with people constantly about the things he was trying to achieve. Some of them had no idea about the subject area, but he said, "The longer I talked to people, I found all of them had something important to impart to me." He continued, "Before I knew it, supportive enthusiastic people, who had the same vision surrounded me with information, documentation, books, guides, and even money." He was admitted into the university. I helped him choose his courses and he advised me on investments.

That conversation with him and with others like him validated my theory of getting the facts first through research and discourse. Research and discourse has never failed me, and right then, I knew it would work for others. It has always worked for me, just as if an angel was in charge of my life, that principal person or thing came into my life to help me complete my journey in every goal. Sometimes it took several years, on other occasions it happened the next day. Nevertheless, that individual or thing would always come into my life and be a prominent figure in my future. That person would describe the activities I needed to complete my vision. Over-time, it became obvious I had planned and achieved my goals with faith, research, and discourse.

Our conversation continued, the student said, "I admit, at first I tried unplanned success. Although I failed, my experiences became more and more helpful, but that initial struggle, trying to make some sense out of my failures made me want to learn more. I was a sad picture of a man completely overcome by fright, due to almost a total lack of preparation." He went on to explain that he thought that only the prepared person deserves to be confident in his or her vision. In short, how can anyone ever hope to storm the fortress of fear if he or she goes into battle with defective weapons or with no ammunition at all? If you want to develop confidence in the fact that you can make your dreams come true, why not do the one thing that will give you security and help you achieve your goals? You must do your research about the subject, develop a plan, and have the faith that discourse will gravitate to you the tools you need.

Incidentally, that student who told me his story of wealth, in the end stated, "I will make a million again because I did it before." With true faith, he was willing to take the risk to achieve his goals, but more importantly to live in joy doing what he loved to do. Sometimes, to go after a better life, you have to take calculated risks, whether that means trying a new job, leaving an unhealthy relationship, or offering yourself as a candidate for a community leadership position.

**(Read Aloud)**
**I will nurture my relationships with my family, friends, and associates.**

It is important that we nurture the abilities of another person. We need to nurture their dreams, and relate to one another from our own vision. We must value his or her abilities by trying to understand their experiences and current responsibilities. As an academic advisor, it seems that every semester a senior in our program needed to enroll in over 18 credit hours to complete their degree. The university assumes that students should not take more than 5 courses, or 15 credit hours per semester. In order for the student to take additional courses, they needed an advisor's and Dean's signature. It is up to the advisor's evaluation of the student's ability to successfully complete the additional coursework to complete the required 120 hours. Long story short, I have single parent students working full-time, taking care of their relatives, and who are enrolled in 18 or more credit hours at the university. Additionally, those same students are taking two additional courses at another university totaling eight classes in their final semester of coursework. Each semester, 98% of those students who needed and believed they were going to graduate that semester achieved their goals and graduated.

I need you to bear in mind, that more or less, all of us have a tendency to underestimate our inner resources, our inner abilities, and we have a difficult time keeping that thought at the center of our awareness; let alone, our ability to nurture the abilities of others. Every-time I step out on faith, I believe that I am capable of doing more than what I was capable of the day before. For me, the problem is how I nur-ture that in others. For example, each year I have a millionaire walk into my office looking to return to school. Many of them had never taken a course at a university before. Many of them had never attended a junior or senior level institution. I remember one individual that had not finished high school, but had made a million dollars rehabilitating real estate. He did go on to earn his GED (General Education Development test). It is also a joy to talk to these individuals because they are true ex-amples of the human spirit, and true faith. All of them had several things in common:

- **they never underestimated their abilities,**
- **they never underestimated their worth, and**
- **they never gave-up on their faith and spirit.**

That was the center of their thought process.

We are capable of more than we believe. If we remain earnest about this, others can acquire this knowledge from us almost infectiously. Acquiring knowledge infectiously is all about Paradigm Processing through all of the forms of discourse we discussed. We can learn, for example, to listen to the people in our lives. I mean really listen – listen to their expressions of feelings even when those feelings are of uncer-tainty and hesitancy. Moreover, we should learn to listen without indulging any desire to lecture or give speeches that closes off those feelings of uncertainty and hesitancy etcetera. because we realize that totally experiencing unwanted feelings is the first step toward going beyond them. Many times when we listen to our inner-voices with a critical assessment, we can see things from a stranger's point of view. We do this so that we will have the answers to those disagreeing and unexpected questions from those pessimistic individuals.

Certainly, we must understand that many people function better with pessimistic discourse. They pay compliments, and then become very discouraging, and that works for some people and in some relationships. It is very selfish of the pessimist because it is emotionally draining and mentally destructive. You must learn to stay away from these people when they are speaking in that manner, because, as you know those pessimistic remarks, and actions affect individuals' short and long-term paradigm, faith, and trust in the human spirit.

**(Read Aloud)**
**I will use my faithfulness to take risks.**

In addition to using the principles of this book in everyday actions, where incidentally you will reap the greatest rewards, you should seek every opportunity to take a risk on yourself. How do you do this? Do not just be an inactive member, or a mere onlooker. Pitch in and help by doing committee work. Get to be a program chairperson or a member of the board of directors. That will give you an opportunity to have discourse in your community, and you certainly will be called upon to donate your time.

As soon as possible, develop a plan to contact people you do not know, but believe would help you get to your goals. Use the suggestions in this book as a guide. If you are not currently a member of a club or organization, go out and research clubs and organizations to join. Join clubs and organizations that fit your new vision of life for you, your community, and your family. Offer your services to a non-for-profit organization in your town. Also, take a risk on fund-raising campaigns that are always looking for volunteers. Joining fund-raising campaigns that will give you that much needed experience in an area that helps you down the line. They provide you with an experiential kit, which will be of great help in preparing you to raise money for your own projects. Many successful people have begun in this way. Some of them have risen to great prominence.

Take the secretary that had a vision of becoming a politician. She took a risk by first volunteering in her community. Just on a whim, she decided to run for an aldermanic position. As a sideline, she began writing letters and opening short talks about what she knew best, her family, her community, her faith, and her concerns about the future of her neighborhood. By volunteering, her dreams and wishes took fire and she was soon voted into office. She took a risk in faith. Her faith, and her joy for helping people took over, which has led her to wealth and personal fulfillment.

**(Read Aloud)**
**I will let people and the universe know where I stand, what I want, all of my needs, and what brings me joy with a loud enthusiasm.**

I met a young man who had lived what some would consider the hard life in the United States. He was an ex-drug addict who had changed his life by creating a paradigm of himself. When I asked how he did it, he replied, "I praised everyday and talked about my visions loudly and proudly with true faith that all of my wishes would come true." When I asked where and when he started, he replied, "I started in prison. I realized that I had done some things that most men will never know, and I did it with true faith, and by taking risks to achieve my visions." He went on to say, "Although it was illegal actions that I envisioned, it was the only way I knew how to reach my goals in my environment and culture. I made millions, had the luxurious homes, newest cars, and met some of the most influential people in the world, but I knew that kind of life was wrong and that I had to change."

He stated that he envisioned his future with true faith, worked hard, and then he put himself in the right location to see his vision through to the end. The interesting thing was what he said next, which made me stand-up. He said, "I started talking aloud to myself about my vision, and then I talked to others." He went on to say that, "Once I was in the right location, and was talking to the universe (to himself) the right people would somehow show-up and be in front of me talking the same language about the same vision."

Nevertheless, he lost it all, the houses, cars, and money, when he went to prison. In prison, he reflected on how he could replicate his vision in the dominant culture, legally. During our discussion, we talked more about the latter part, which was praise, talking to himself, discourse with others, true faith, enthusiasm and gravitating interest. He talked about how in prison he would experiment with his new found reality. A reality where he could gravitate any and everything he wanted to himself with self-discourse, and discourse with others.

When he was released from prison, he continued enthusiastic praise, i.e., self-discourse, true faith, and hard work to achieve his goal of starting a for-profit business and a non-profit organization that helped ex-offenders. He enrolled in classes at the local university where he devoted most of his time to discourse with others about his goals, visions, and aspirations.

In school, he hastily and exhaustively assembled facts from books written by religious philosophical and motivational authors. For him, the books confirmed his positive idealistic reality that he had created for himself in prison. The literature confirmed the connection between his past, present, and future. Although he had lived in places, and times where he was homeless, did not eat some days, sold and did illegal drugs, he did not and could not envision one personal instance of why thinking and speaking positively, with loud enthusiasm would not guarantee a positive future. He merely let people and the universe know where he stood, what he wanted, all of his needs, and what would bring him joy with loud enthusiasm, praise, and gratitude.

Our talk was about the transformation of a young man from homelessness to illegal riches, from prison to self-enlightenment, and finally to loud enthusiastic joy and legal riches. Our initial discourse was as distressing for me to hear, as it was agonizing for him to give until he got to the end where praise and joy took over his life. He stated that, "It is impossible for me to feel badly about my past because for me it was that experience that has afforded me the opportunity to help so many people today." From this example, it is my hope that you will become curious about your life, about your joy, and about your experiences.

As I have pointed out repeatedly, you cannot help but succeed if you choose to live in joy, positive thought, and actions with convictions. Right now, I am sure that you have some strong beliefs about some aspect of your life that makes you special-that makes your experiences unique. You do not have to search deep into your mental database for those experiences – they generally lie on the surface of your stream of consciousness, because you often think about them. You have always thought about your experiences and how things would have been different had you been more inquisitive about your ideas.

**(Read Aloud)**
**I will be inquisitive about life and all that it has to offer.**

Not long ago, I was facilitating an online (WEB base) course at the university, an assignment that I had assigned to the students was writing his or her obituary. The idea is that a self-written obituary would indicate how he or she believed they contributed to society and how society had viewed them. I believe the way we view our lives shapes our future, which can be seen through our experience. Conversely, the way we see what is accessible to us via communication and information determines who we are and what we are to do in life.

How you characterize life is established by your paradigm, and your perception on life. Your paradigm will influence how you dedicate your time, spend your money, use your talents or genius, and how you value your relationships. One of the best ways to understand another individual's paradigm, or view of him or herself is to ask them, "What would your obituary say about you?" On-one-hand, you will determine that there are as many different answers to that question as there are people on earth. On-the-other-hand, you will determine that his or her answers are related to their cultural norms, values, economic circumstance, and political ideology.

After they completed the assignment, I asked, was this the life you wanted for yourself from childhood? Ninety-nine percent of the people I asked that question indicated that they had changed to be less than what they envisioned. They responded with quotes like the following: "He was a good provider, and a good person," or "He was always on time and never complained," or "He was a hard worker, and a loyal friend," or "She made life so enjoyable, and withstood all of the troubles that came her way," – which are all good testimonials. However, that is not living life to the fullest; the potential, or the recognition that we envision for ourselves early on in life.

One thing that I noticed, when I asked the question, was that many individual dreams had been changed to just exist. Their paradigm had been processed to work in a society (e.g., the United States of America) where the people are supposed to live out their dreams. The other 1% believed their obituary would say something like this, "He was a visionary and a person who decided that life was more than just being alive. For him, life was an extravaganza, a rollercoaster, an enigma, a symphony, a journey, and he danced to the beat of life with so much success and joy."

The second question was, after writing and reading your obituary, I asked, "How do you picture your life now, what image would come to your mind? That image should be a renewed vision of life. Because of that Paradigm Processing exercise a Paradigm Shift generally occurred, a new paradigm, a new vision. They became inquisitive about life again and all that it has to offer. With understanding, visions changed from just existing, to true joy and a true belief that life is suppose to be about being successful. A success driven life that varies differently among the individual, that could be processed to fit any society, or any reality, regardless of age. It is this view of life that you will hold on to after consciously observing what people thought about your life after death or how others have seen you throughout life's journey so far.

# Chapter 17

## *What makes an educated person?*

One of the questions that I like to ask the individuals that take my courses, attend my presentations, or seminars is, "What makes an educated person? One thing that I found to be interesting was that over 15% believed that being formally educated is the only form of education. These individuals stated that he or she is not educated unless he or she has attended a college or university. Now, 98% of the individuals questioned were working and over the age of 25. Another 25% stated that experience determined if a person was educated. Many individuals stated that, "You have to do it to learn." In the end however, I found that 60% of the individuals questioned, believed that education could only be obtained through trial and error, or inquisitive discovery.

No one person should think that there is no more knowledge for him or her to gain after a formal education. Additionally, he or she should not fear what comes from inquisitive discovery, nor fear the outcome of that discovery. The depth of human intellect is not just measured by the theories gained from others through formal education. The works of human beings over the years have been mastered through inquisitive discovery, which helped to create the theories and practices human beings now exercise. The highest, deepest, and broadest flight of the imagination can be found from inquisitive discovery.

There is time, without end, beyond all that we can comprehend from discovery, and imagination. We can see it in our relationships with others and especially in popular culture. We have seen only the glimmering of what can be discovered from the multitude of knowledge and wisdom that is constantly being developed. In the same way, the riches of the world will come to him or her who will dig for it. No one can dig deep into the mind without the need to discover the rewards that could be; from completing the process from imagination to reality; to fulfill that need to discover how deep and how far the imagination would take them, and the rewards that will follow. When men and women are willing to be instructed as if they were a little child with complete faith, when he or she submits to his or her imagination of what could be with courage conviction, and fearless inquisitive discovery, only then will they receive all of the rewards. In other words, if men and women would be obedient to their feelings and emotions about inquisitive discovery and true to the gifts that they were born with, and the gifts that were bestowed to them throughout life, they will achieve their dreams and goals. By doing this, he or she will understand how everything that they need has been, and will continue to be provided to them.

The blissful world that I am trying to process for you would open its chambers of riches when you believe that you can achieve anything with inquisitive discovery and can achieve any goal. For example, one day I met a beautiful woman who had unbelievable charisma, but was unaware of her ability to speak in public, to motivate, and change lives with her words. She had not discovered the gift that was bestowed to her. I think I was the first person to tell her that she had this great gift.

One day, this beautiful woman decided to share with me a book that she had been thinking about writing. It was a fiction urban novel and she wanted my opinion. That day was a day of self-discovery, but that discovery was short lived because she was not willing to be instructed with "childlike" faith. That wonderful day, I discovered that she had been given a great gift. Everyday that we were together, I wanted to hear the next chapter, the next paragraph, the next sentence, and the next word. She had me captivated by the words she put on paper, and the way she told the story.

It was the beginning of the best book I had ever read, which was never finished with its captivating storyline and intriguing dialog. That's right; she stopped writing the book because she did not believe in our discovery. That book was never given to the public for its enrichment, it never made the world a better place, and her talents were placed in limbo by her lack of true faith, courage and conviction, and inquisitive discovery.

Nevertheless, today that beautiful woman has earned her Master of Arts Degree in Professional Technical Writing, and English. She has books all over the world, and she speaks to large crowds of people all over the world. I know because I married her. Because she has so much to offer the world, I devoted my life to making sure that her talents would be recognized by the world, and I know that the world is a better place with her in it.

The point is, human beings from the cradle to the grave would be altogether different had they believed in what others may have seen in them. For example, most children never listen to their parents until they are in trouble, or experienced something traumatic and really need their help. For the adult, the question becomes, "What is the mystery of deliverance from missed opportunities?" One way is to change your thought process to create a paradigm that is positive and spreads through positive discourse.

**(Read Aloud)**
**I will be curious about life and all that it has to offer me.**

You may say, as I said to one of my mentees who was searching for the joy of life, "You have to be curious about life. You have no strong convictions or interests right now. What is it that you want out of life? Why are you here?" I am always a little surprised at this, but I told this

**127**

mentee to get curious, to get busy, and to get motivated about something. "What, for instance?" he asked. "What are you interested in?" I asked. He continued. "Well, I've always wanted to have my own business." "Doing what?" I asked. "Well, I haven't thought about that yet." "Well, when do you plan on thinking about it?" With a strange look on his face he said, "I guess I plan to think about it right now." I smiled because I was happy that he was ready to take control of his dream. I said, "Writing government grants would be a good place to start?" He asked in a bewildered tone. "What are grants?" I told him, "State and Federal grants. It's money set aside by the government for people who have aspirations to step out on their own – to pursue their dreams. Go on the World Wide Web (www) and search for State and Federal grants – all of the information that you need is right at your fingertips. When you are done come back and we will talk about them." He did.

When he came back, there was no holding him down. He started to talk about how he could write a grant on the State and Federal level that would give him money to pay for school and an opportunity to finance his dream. It was as if he had a new toy, he spoke with eagerness and impatience, "A method to obtain free money to go to school, for housing and for a business. Wow!" When I tried to stop him, he began to talk uncontrollably about the 25 books and WEB sites on government and private grants that he had found, and he had read it all. I was pleased that he took an opportunity to search that which will give him joy – set him on a new path and a new journey.

Here is another suggestion: become curious about what you now consider a good topic or about what would bring you joy throughout the rest of your life. The more you know about something the more earnest and excitedly enthusiastic you will become. Never stop learning about what you want out of life, what you enjoy, how you feel, and how to make your life better. If you have ever had the opportunity to sell something for someone, the first thing they tell you to do is to learn everything you can about the product before you sell it. In other words, the more you know, or are curious about, the more enthusiastic you become about it. The same thing is true about your joy – the more you know about what makes you happy, the more earnest and enthusiastic you will be about it.

For example, I remember the time I was curious about the power in prayer, the power of believing in God. Through my research, I found that believing in God, and things unseen, actually begins with you; believing in prayer and God, is believing that anything is possible, even the possibility that God can cure your disease, change your present situation, and create positive changes in your life.

A sad thing occurred during my research. My father had a heart attack and drifted into a coma. Now, my father was a highly religious man who attended church every Wednesday for Bible study, and every Sunday for service. While my father was in intensive care at the hospital, a pastor from the church he attended came to see him. At that time, I was the only person sitting in the room with my father. My father was still sedated and about to go to surgery for a heart procedure when the minister entered the room. My father had tubes in his throat, and many wires attached to his chest and other vital organs. All of the tubes and wires provided information that could be seen through a monitoring machine that sat near the top of his bed.

The pastor grabbed my father's hand with his right hand and held my hand in his left hand. He began to pray. As he prayed, we noticed the wavelengths on the brain-monitoring machine began to speed up indicating brain activity. It was as if my father could hear us. It was as if the prayer created pure energy. I know it did because I could feel it flowing through my body. When the pastor stopped praying the wavelengths on the monitor slowed down and went back to normal, and when we started praying again the wavelengths sped up. My father was unconscious and heavily sedated. How could this be happening?

In that moment, the prayer with the Pastor and my father was truly electrifying and energetic. I believed God gave me a lesson of his existence. I believe God tunneled deep into my mind and soul. I believe He showed me in that instance that He is real, that prayer creates its own energy, and its own reality of what is not now, really is, and what is not seen now, does exist in the future. Believing in God and prayer imparts power that gives human beings the mastery of him or herself, it brings every impulse and passion within our nature under the control of a higher power, it is being curious about the unseen, and is pure positive mental energy. It makes the possessor of this power the owners of everything that is possible on earth. It brings him or her into communion with pure energy and the mind of the infinite, and it opens to him or her to the rich treasures in any given space, place, or time. This is knowledge that cannot be obtained by researching the word of God in all religions, but by God teaching valuable lessons in prayer that is found in every soul who will take a risk to obtain it.

# Chapter 18

*What is the one educated faithful risk that you could take today that would move you efficiently and effectively toward fulfilling your vision of a better life?*

One educated faithful risk that you could take today and everyday could demonstrate how important it is to show worth and nobility to others, which creates a paradigm of worth for you. However, to do this you must conquer the mind to learn the strategies of thinking positively and acting with a sense of nobility.

I think the best example of thinking positively and being a faithful risk-taker would be the movie entitled, *Forrest Gump. Forrest Gump* is the movie of a man who by today's standard is considered mentally handicap but, on the other hand, was he? Yes, his IQ was 87, but his ability to gravitate wealth, people, and love to him was at the level of a genius. As I watched the movie, I noticed that Mr. Gump accepted and took a risk on every opportunity that was presented to him. Not only did he accept the gifts, he embraced them. First, he wanted to go to college to earn his degree, and he did. There, he earned a spot on the local university football team where he became an All American. Because of his All American status, he met the President of the United States. After college, he was offered an opportunity to go into the military, and he did. He did not know what would happen; he just took a risk in faith. In the end, he accomplished more than many of us ever would; because of your unwillingness to take a chance, you never will.

**(Read aloud)**
**I will not judge anyone, and I will respect everyone as long as I am being respected.**

While each of us are ultimately responsible for his or her paradigm and thinking, we have the choice of accepting the gifts of life with self-confidence and self-respect. If you want to be successful in anything that you do, you have to treat people with respect. Respect anyone you have discourse and/or transactions with, just as others have that choice in their communications with you. Almost certainly, all of us can think of instances when someone dealt with us in a way that acknowledged our worth. Not only did he or she acknowledge your worth, but they acknowledged their worth in the process. Moreover, we can remember incidences when someone dealt with us as if we had "stolen something from their mother." We know the difference in how those two kinds of experiences feel. I am sure we all would prefer the times we dealt with someone in a spirit of mutual worth. In addition, we can probably recall occasions when, out of fear, hurt or anger, we decided to change the direction of a discussion from calmness to anger, at that moment nobility, and dignity loses all meaning for us.

When our interactions, whether through discourse or hearsay, have worth and are noble, in the end, those interactions are more enjoyable. When we manifest worth to others, we like ourselves more. When we act in ways that encourage the worth of others, we sustain our own worth and nobility. I have seen and heard lecturers, counselors, mentors, and advisors who have had a deep impact on people just by treating them with a sense of worth. If we appreciate some of the most important distinctiveness of how these cultivators of the mind relate to people, we can apply the principles to our own interactions.

There is nothing mysterious about this knowledge. Ideally, it should be available to everyone. My personal wish is that one day it will be taught to schoolchildren. I have questioned higher education students many times in order to learn which behaviors of mine were most helpful in strengthening their sense of worth. Certain themes recurred repeatedly. None of them were unique to me. The behaviors I am about to describe, illustrates how to facilitate the growth of nobility and worth in students.

To begin, we take care of human beings from the basis of value. This, for me, is the first imperative of effective facilitation of the human spirit. This is illustrated in how I greet students when they arrive in the office:

- **effective eye communication;**
- **being non-patronizing;**
- **being conscientious;**
- **being appropriately spontaneous;**
- **attentively paying attention;**
- **being perceptive, and**
- **understanding.**

Taking care of human beings entails such matters as courtesy and making sure that he or she is being understood. The message that I am conveying is that human beings are an entity deserving of worth and respect. However, we fail to realize how important it is to maintain that sense of worth and nobility in our own lives. The risk we take to treat others with a sense of worth and nobility requires believing that you can be a sign of hope to someone else.

**(Read Aloud)**
**I will not be fearful or insecure when taking risks that show worth and nobility to others.**

A young woman once said to me, "Looking back over our talks during our advising sessions, I feel that nothing else that happened at this institution was quite as impactful as the simple fact that I always felt respected by you, and that you did not act like someone too busy to understand my concerns or my needs. I said everything I could to make you talk me into quitting school; the lack of a job, my children, and especially my math phobia. I kept trying to give you a reason to get me to quit school. You refused to cooperate. Somehow, I had to deal with all of the things that were going on in my life, which was difficult at first, but as I considered all of your ideas and wisdom, it began to take hold. I remembered that at one of our first sessions, I said, My father would talk to any busboy with more courtesy than he ever showed to me. I felt worthless around him. It was painful and it angered me to the point where I wanted to make trouble just for some form of affection. You helped me to understand that now is the time to take care of me. I am grateful that you didn't give up on me."

When a student, or a person in general, young or old, is describing feelings of worthlessness, fear, pain, or anger, it is not helpful to respond with, "Oh, you should not feel that way." Your role is not only that of a cheerleader, but also a person who leads with courage and conviction, truth and honesty. You have to be a leader willing to show your feelings while bluntly talking about situations where you have wisdom and real world experience that is similar to theirs.

There is great value in expressing feelings without having to deal with a persons' analysis, blame, mockery, or criticism. The process of expressing feelings is often fundamentally therapeutic. As a person taking a risk on relationship building through discourse, you have to be able to project your worth by sincerely listening with empathy, which is the basis of bringing out the feelings of worth in others. It is also the basis to authenticate friendship, to say nothing of love. Contrast this with relationships where people are constantly interrupting you with sermons or advice or a change of subject when you attempt to communicate powerful emotions; as if you are surrounded by people who had very little confidence in you or in themselves.

I regard one of my first tasks to be that of a person willing to create an atmosphere where the person can express their thoughts and opinions without fear of ridicule or criticism. In all of your relationships and interactions, ask yourself whether you have created an atmosphere of honesty or selfishness. As you know, in an environment of selfishness, people lose trust in you and your worth.

One of the experiences that people can hope for in any relationship is that of being visible – seen and understood. Perhaps they have felt unworthy of respect and were overlooked since childhood, and they long for a different sense of themselves. This is with respect to a person feeling unworthy to the yearning and understanding of him or herself as a legitimate intelligent human being. In taking a risk on your own worth, seek to respond appropriately by sharing experiences about yourself and providing feedback that allows individuals to feel a part of your life. You might want to say things like, I think I hear you saying...I imagine you might be feeling...right now you look as if...let me tell you how I understand your viewpoint...etcetera.

However, this is human discourse, not merely a computer just transmitting data and information. We all long for the experience of feeling worthy and heard. Effective people in effective relationships that are mutually faithfully dependable do judge one another, but are not judgmental. They judge one another in that they clearly consider various behaviors as unique to others from the point of view of the long-term happiness and well-being of the relationship. They are not as deceitful as to make-believe that they are without principles or without likes and dislikes. However, they do not lecture and they do not seek to change their conduct by inducing guilt trips that eventually erode the relationship until it is unfaithful and untrusting. Accordingly, individuals in reciprocal worth building relationships do overestimate their influence. For instance, I had a student in my program that was an alcoholic and yet was a good student. Higher education is more than just showing up

**135**

for class, and doing the work. It is the ability to collaborate and cohabitate with staff, administration, faculty, and fellow students. There is a certain amount of trust, and faith in producing leaders through higher education. In other words, his drinking problem was a problem for the institution of higher education. I did not say, "I cannot help you until you do something about your drinking problem." However, I did with courage and conviction, advised him not to attend. You could not attend some events where he interacted with people that could someday help him – at least not now.

When we overwhelm individuals with our assessment of who they are or their abilities, we will bully them into creating an environment that would not inspire growth, worth, trust, faith, or self-respect. Alternatively, you should not have a policy of showering individuals with compliments and excessive admiration. That conversation would often strengthen thoughts of unworthiness (or invisibility) if the beneficiary of the admiration knows that you're being complimentary and not precise. In other words, they believe that you are lying about their worth. I remember when I first thought about going back to school to earn my doctorate. I was working with a young man who I praised for working toward his doctorate. As I praised him, he began to give information on how I could do what he was doing to earn my doctorate. The praise was reciprocated with praise and information, because it was honest and both of us knew it.

We can learn to say what we like or dislike, admire or do not admire, without labeling, assaulting, or praising idealistically. In my experience, being inspirational, compassionate, and not emotional would encourage more than discourage. A large number of my students, especially my adult students, have mentioned the significance of this difference during their progress in higher education. Many of my adult students have come to me saying that they cannot do this or that because they had been out of school for over ten or twenty years, it will be difficult. I would ask, "What do you think you might do to change your mindset or improve your situation? What actions are you willing to take?" A change usually comes when these questions will need to be asked and dealt with. I believe that part of my job consists of awakening people to an action orientation, which answers those questions. Action orientations improve current situations, and are generally actions that can be taken now. In dealing with people in general there will inevitably be times when you can help them, if we choose to, by conveying just a perspective of inspiring growth, worth, trust, faith, or self-respect for one another.

Effective people that are on a quest to continue to grow in faith are kind, but they do not let individuals walk all over them or disrespect them. With courage and conviction, they do not. For example, by continuing to tolerate individuals calling on you at any hour of the day or night over trivial matters is disrespectful of you and your time. You cannot allow individuals to be emotionally, as well as, monetarily oppressive at all. You must believe that helping number one (themselves) is actually helping number two (fellow man/woman).

**(Read Aloud)**
**Thinking only of yourself will only cause a rift in the relationship. My time is valuable.**

Effective people value their time, and they require that the value of their time be recognized. I remember a student who was a hair-stylist by trade who told me that she was having problems with a family member who did not want to pay for her services as a hair professional. She had to pay for her books, children to feed, a house, and a grandmother she was taking care of. She was very distressed because they wanted to continue to receive her services without paying for it. Her close family members were not talking to her because she was styling their hair freely when she was in cosmetology school. However, now that she has graduated, and was continuing her education at a higher education institution, they had to pay to get their hair styled. They wanted to continue to receive her services without pay. She could not afford to freely give her time any longer so she decided to let them know that her time was valuable and that they needed to respect that. She stated that the un-insulting conversation freed her from the mental stress and demoralizing feeling of being used.

Effective people do not leave individuals in an insulting manner or with hostility, but with reasoning and justification (unless it had to be done immediately with courage and conviction because sometimes it is healing). Effective people are very good at creating ground rules for their lives. They set restrictions on what they except from other people in relationships. It is what good parents call "tough love". Acting in this way is intelligent, self-respecting, and important to your health, needs, and valuable time. To be effective in your relationships, you have to set the example. The example you set says to others that, this is how, I treat myself and this is how you should treat yourself. Therefore, there is no conflict relating to what can be considered realistic self-interest (honorable respect for one's own interests) on one hand and healthy loving relationship building on the other.

This ideology of building healthy loving relationships is important to those of us working to maintain healthy "wealthy" associations. It is the same as those of us that are parents going to school, working two jobs, missing out on special occasions, essentially self-sacrificing to the point where we as parents give up our lives for our children and elderly parents. Now, that type of sacrificing does not holistically set a good example, but can merely teach their children that it is improper to regard themselves as objects of sacrifice without knowing when enough is enough. If you do not know when that point is reached with courage and conviction, you can generate resentment, hatred, and guilt in your children.

The same goes for self-sacrificing relatives, associates, students, and friends, which are a burden, not a joy or an inspiration, or an example of anything positive we want to learn. Those relationships with relatives, associates, students, and friends will generate resentment, hatred, and guilt in you; not being the recipient of the sacrifice. I remember working at the Board of Trade in downtown Chicago. At this particular company, employees could volunteer to work overtime on Saturdays. There was always this one particular person who always volunteered. She sacrificed time with her children and family. I asked her why she volunteered all of the time and she said, "That she was hoping to get a management position." Her supervisor was a friend and felt that as a result of her sacrifices for the company that her friend would be obligated to give her the position, but that did not happen. Her sacrifice turned an excellent relationship into one where resentment, guilt, and hatred ruled.

**(Read Aloud)**
**I will be more sensitive to human behaviors.**

I am very much sensitive to the behaviors of human beings, including the most undesirable behavior. As-a-matter-of-fact, I think we all are. I think we have the ability to truly and deeply feel when behavior is about to be undesirable. On some level, undesirable behavior has worth and value, it tells a story. For example, a wife's angry shrieking, which may be very unpleasant to witness, makes its own kind of sense if we know that nothing less has ever caught her husband's attention. Maybe she has no sense of an alternative way of doing things that would work better. In other words, what he sees in his wife's actions is very different to what others identify with. If we do not understand a person and merely label him or her as strange, we need to know the background in which the person's manners makes some kind of logic, which includes, "Was the impressions desirable or even necessary," even if objectively it is totally irrational.

**139**

On the level of our personal relationships, this means helping a person who is behaving inappropriately to identify where he or she is coming from. For instance, that secretary that always has an attitude, that teller that has an evil look on his or her face when she or he is giving you your money, or that supervisor who is always giving you a problem. To grasp what needs are trying to be satisfied, we must try to apply diplomacy first and then understand that none of this is about you or anything that you may or may not have done, but something beyond you. In other words, we want to offer that person understanding and compassion before making a final decision about their character or their behavior. Obviously, we cannot practice this policy equally with every individual we come across. However, with people we love or really care about or perhaps people we work with, it is a powerful tool. In many occasions, it is just a part of this ideal of Identity Socialization and needed for continued growth both internally and externally.

# Chapter 19

## *Know your society!*

According to Doob (1994), "Socialization is a progression where participants are concerned with values and beliefs that are passed on to participants in that society, a process by which a person becomes a social being, learning the necessary cultural content and behavior to become a member of a group or society." Therefore, if we do not understand a person's culture and social identity, and label him or her, we may create incredible remorse and stress in relationships. Just because we do not understand an individual's paradigm or relationship to their culture, does not mean we have to judge them.

Paradigms and relationships can be affected by our physical and emotional actions directly or indirectly, verbally or nonverbally, overtly or covertly (Kuhn, 1962; Huene-Hoyningen, 1993; Dietze, 2001). The Socialization Paradigm Process transpires through the observation of modes, sequences, and styles of behavior during interactions with individuals we are exposed to on a daily basis.

Modeling of behaviors and exposure to culturally relevant materials and activities are some of the methods that we can use to build better connections with people from different cultures, sub-cultures, and age groups. One example would be the deep-rooted theory of the affects of popular culture on paradigms (i.e., televisions, WEB, and magazines) that we read and react to. People react to popular culture by changing their behavior such as by changing the way that they dress, or by using popular words such as "Groovy" of the 80's, or "Word" of the 90's.

The implication is that Paradigm Processing from popular culture affects available options and chances of succeeding educationally, economically, socially, and politically. Popular culture is often progressive and older more established cultural traits take longer to Paradigm Process to the new Paradigm Shift. For example, many years ago men in the United States would not have been seen wearing earrings. Wearing earrings was something that only women would wear. Nowadays, men wear earrings to job interviews, which was a Paradigm Shift from the past. However, when men first started wearing earrings many of them was seen as weird. Nonetheless, years ago no man would ever be seen wearing earrings to a job interview. Men did not start wearing earrings to job interviews until the interviewers started wearing earrings, which was a Paradigm Shift. Still, the process of wearing earrings to job interviews was not complete until it was accepted by all interviewers. When members outside of a paradigm finally gave up and arrived in the next paradigm not much may had seemed to change, but it had. Those people wearing earrings to the interview have a better chance of getting that job or raise now that there has been a paradigm shift.

Those outside of this "professional" collective will find it difficult to pass through this well-maintained opposed society and environment set by the older United States' collective. Specifically, a society and environment that makes it difficult for the acquisition of a good job, a good education, and/or a good place to live, a cultural environment that controls who, what, where and how success is achieved. In other words, for every action there is a reaction (Dietze, 2001; Beauboeuf et el., 1996).

The reaction to changes in popular culture affects social outcomes, and more importantly psychological perceptions. For example, television shows, movies, and magazines, make women feel fat and unattractive. While those same tools of popular culture says to men, it's okay to be a little overweight, drink beer, and sit around watching sports. I think popular culture affects women differently than it affects men. Many women have told me that women dress for women, not for men. Women care about what women think of what they have on rather than what men think of their attire. Therefore, women are constantly looking to popular culture for validation. Men look to popular culture for items that attract women, e.g., cars, large luxurious homes, and/or tools to fix them. Popular culture helps to drive our economic, psychological perception, and our view of the world. The ideology of popular culture is socialization and utilitarian, in that it also relates to diverse economic and psychological perceptions. Socialization also relates to differences from the dominant culture in society's social philosophy and the interactions and unions of subcultures.

However, in time, a whole attribute is advanced to an additional Paradigm Shift. In the event that the new paradigm does not intersect with the old paradigm, people in the old paradigm will not be able to move forward into the new concepts and the new paradigm.

**(Read Aloud)**
**I understand that my consciousness and state of being can change for the best.**

The idea is that paradigms act similar to congruent worlds and dimensions, which are the connection between these "worlds" causing other Paradigm Shifts through time, space, discourse and popular culture, which overtime will diminish and then return through historical discourse. For example, when we talk about Paradigm Processing we are talking about traveling between Dimensional shifts. A dimension is a state of being; a personification that increase or decrease the body's capability of attaining more room.

- The Zero Dimension has no length, no breadth, no height, no area and no volume. It is nothing but a point.

- The first dimension is a straight line that engulfs an infinite number of other points – like a point, it also cannot be drawn, but only located, and it also has no mass as it occupies no volume.

- The Second Dimension is any plain figure drawn on a sheet of paper that is represented as a figure; it has area, and is located. However, it has no mass as it occupies no volume. It has two important characteristics:
  - ➤ Length
  - ➤ Breadth

A Two Dimensional Figure may be in any direction on the plane on which it is lying, but it can never leave its plane (i.e. no upward or downward motion).

- The Third Dimension is points and straight lines we physically sketch. What we sketch on a paper is the Three Dimensional mark of graphite or ink; it has length, breadth, height, surface area and volume. The Third Dimension is applying length, breadth, height, surface area and volume to a Two Dimensional square.
  - ➤ The motion of a Three Dimensional 'solid' may be to:
    - Its left side;
    - Its right side;
    - Upwards;
    - Downwards;
    - Forwards;
    - Backwards

- **It has no particular plane of existence, but exists over and through an infinite number of planes.**

According to Ke Akua, A. & Apollo, A., (2007), a 3rd to 4th Dimensional Shift can be looked at as a transcending of the mind, an awakening of an awareness that accepts time as being relative. On this dimensional layer, this experience may not be understood, nor may its origin even be perceived, it is simply felt. Our relationship to all existence unfolds through the language of consciousness in the 4th Dimension, and when we learn this language, we begin to discover perfect patterns inherent within every "conversation," that takes us to the 5th Dimension of consciousness, or that recognition of divine will, and the communion with your spiritual self. On this dimensional layer, we begin to recognize that we are not only connected to others in a very physical sense through the air, atoms, and electrons in the universe, within and throughout space-time, in that our actions ripple through the air as quickly as discourse. We begin to recognize that our voices resonate both inside of time, and outside of the boundaries of matter. Our ideas can be shared instantaneously, and our actions perceived physically, even by those who are thousands of miles away. We even begin to see how visions, actions, and discourse in the distant past can affect us in the present. It is our spiritual center, which unfolds through our awareness of the spiritual fabric of space-time. This awareness gives us a sense of the existence, of pure energy and we suddenly feel the flow of the universe in its many transformations. This feeling allows us to directly relate to our emotions, and deepens our faith in the spiritual. We begin to tune into the frequency changes of others, both in our local space and in distant places. This is a transition of great vulnerability and transparency, and is a powerful point of choice when one decides to either remain open, honest, and transparent, or cloak themselves in the shadows, trying to hide what is within them from others, and often from themselves.

The 6th Dimensional consciousness understands that the entire universe is based on love, and that this love is a creative and supportive element that seeks the "highest good" of all. The energy of love always "imprints" our intentions as creators and supports our creations, whether positive or negative. At the 6th dimension the consciousness is both self-aware and wise enough to monitor its creations and to ensure that it creates from a place of love, joy and abundance. The 6th Dimensional creative energy rests in the wisdom of the 5th Dimension, but encompasses the joyous certainty of the upward evolutionary spiral back to the spiritual. The 7th Dimensional or celestial consciousness, and all further Dimensional awakenings are actually facets of its Eternal Unfolding, and always related to a higher-harmonic level of one of the lower Dimensional centers. The 8th Dimensional consciousness is simply a bridge between these experiences of awareness in the past and future. The 9th Dimensional consciousness links the past and future back into the eternal present, weaving every experience ever had into every experience being created in the eternal self. The 10th Dimensional consciousness once again bridges the eternal self with the eternal mystery of the other, while the 11th Dimensional awareness begins to identify and define that mysterious other into an actual eternal presence and being. The 12th Dimensional consciousness connects back to the 6th, where interaction with that being is experienced in time, and the 13th begins to unify the experience in time through mental perception...and so on and so forth, cycling back through each of the basic principles activating multiple layers simultaneously.

**(Read Aloud)**
**I have greater potential than I realized.**

Time and historical discourse is very important because it eliminates the remorse of past actions toward the new discourse. Remember that remorse does not serve anyone's interests, and, in saying this, there is no implication of biased accounts over wrongdoing or of sponsoring indifferences. There are obviously times when we need to say, your behavior is completely unacceptable to me. For many it is very difficult, especially when that unacceptable behavior is toward a different culture, ideology, or race from the dominant culture and social norms. For example, it is the equivalent of judging someone based on their age, gender, and the color of their skin. My goal is to induce a behavioral change by changing paradigms in the way we indulge in our relationships with one another regardless of the differences.

One unique ability between an ineffective and effective leader is that they know that the people they lead have greater potential than they recognize. For example, I would ask students, "What is it that you can do today to become wealthy? Do you believe you can become wealthy?" About 95% of the adults would say, "I believe I can become wealthy, but I do not know how." I would say, "I believe you can too." And, "Do you think you need people?" Most of the people I interviewed stated, "Yes, I need people, but I don't trust people." I asked, "Can you learn to trust people?" "Yes," most people said."

**(Read Aloud)**
**I will trust people, because I need people.**

To learn to trust people you must:

- **Trust yourself.**
  - ➤ **When you feel that something is wrong, it is probably wrong.**

**147**

➤ When you feel that something is right, take a risk in faith and make a difference.

• Trust in your spirit.
  ➤ Accept the gift that your spirit will gravitate to you.

• Be grateful.
  ➤ Express thanks constantly
    • To others, and
    • In the spirit

• Speak to everybody.
  ➤ Speak even if he or she does not return the gesture.

• Do for others without expectance.
  ➤ Give at your church
    • Donate to homeless shelters and charities

• Volunteer in your community.
  ➤ Help the elderly
  ➤ Feed the homeless
  ➤ Review cover letters and resumes for those trying to get back into the work force, or
  ➤ Coach in your community, etcetera

As a coach, you can help the children in your community to:
• Become leaders,
• Learn teamwork,
• Learn emotional control, and
• Learn the importance of health and physical fitness, etcetera

As a little league baseball coach myself, I would ask the players, "Do you think you can hit the baseball better, catch the ball better, or run faster? If not, why not? If the players thought that he could not, I would find someone who could run faster than he could, and then say, "Try again." If I was not motivating them on the field, I was teaching them how to change their mindset. I remember one player who could not hit the ball in a game, but was one of my best batting cage hitters. The fact that he could not get a hit in a game was all in his head. I never told him that. I would tell him and his father that he was going to start hitting just when his team needed it the most.

It was the playoffs and if we lost one game, our season would be over. During the playoffs, that young man could not miss the baseball. He hit every ball that was in his hitting zone. The point is that I did not allow my players to buy into harmful negative depictions of themselves. Everything was positive, even the mistakes they made. Mistakes were learning experiences used for practice. This is a point of the highest importance. Mistakes are a part of life and the learning process.

As a new advisor at the university, I asked one of my associates, "What factors were the most responsible for his success as an advisor." He stated, "I would rank my success by a student's ability to earn their degree doing something that he or she enjoyed doing." He went on to say, "I would start by ranking the students' harmful negative depictions of themselves and secondly, I would rank success by the following statements made by a student: "I did not think I could ever earn a living at something I really enjoyed. Now, I am doing it. I never could picture myself making enough money to support my family. Now, I am." Or, "I did not think I could take and pass that many courses to graduate, and yet I did."

# Chapter 20

*Refuse to participate in discourse with a pessimist because when we are rational, harmonious, and trustworthy, our own feelings of worth yields a profitable return.*

We have to refuse to participate in discourse with a pessimist. Ask him or her, "I wonder what you get out of being a naysayer, a worrywart, or a gloomy Gus?" It can be very difficult to maintain a relationship when that relationship is strained with pessimistic discourse. The good thing is that we can decline that person's request for negative dialog, and explain why. That would be one of the greatest gifts we can offer those individuals who have cynic characteristics. We will always succeed in changing that paradigm of pessimistic safeguarding. It is safe because they can always say, "I told you so" or "I am glad I was wrong." Nonetheless, we can only try to change these individuals before you let them go with courage and conviction. Optimally, we want to bring out the best within the other person. At bare minimum, we will strengthen the best in ourselves.

To whatever level we are rational, harmonious, and trustworthy in our discourse with people; we offer them a plain and logical sense of truth. Moreover, any person trying to build better relationships and paradigms of him or her strives to offer this judgment in his or her discourse with others. We have been discussing that it would take getting everyone involved to get to this idea of holistic wealth, and any positive self-respecting human would strive to make that happen. Thus, we signal to those pessimistic individuals you are intelligent and capable in dealing with me positively and confidently.

I am not presenting a "maze-like" ideology of ideals of success by thinking and acting positively. I am saying be positive about everything, and control your emotions toward opposing ideas of certainty such as those that would leave you feeling baffled, incapable, and weak. When we are rational, harmonious, and trustworthy, our own feelings of worth yields a profitable return. Those interpretations of the connections between individuals are appropriately even to our discourse with adults more than with children. Since I explored the subject, from my experiences, I shall not cover that ground again here. What I am outlining are the common rules related to all of our relationships. However, if you have children, go over the previous metaphors and examples of interactions and connections between them and their behaviors and consider how constantly you follow through on them, since children require these behaviors from you even more than adults do.

I actually believe that my mother was responsible for me being confident and self-encouraging. As a child, I had the experience of being respected, she believed in me, and she constantly conveyed that belief. She made me feel like my feelings mattered. My individuality did not go un-nurtured, it was fed. I have heard numerous successful people say that their parents did the same for them. Many sociologists have researched this area and believe that parents, who nurture, learn to attend to their children's unique needs by building positive relationships with them, and by sending consistent messages of love and support (Smith, et al., 1994). Parents, like my mother, express affection and compassion, foster self-respect, and hope. They always listen and attend to their children's feelings and ideas; teach kindness and giving to those less fortunate, and provide for their nutrition, shelter, clothing, health and safety. They celebrate life with their children; help them feel connected to their

**151**

family's history and cultural heritage (Smith et al., 1994).

**(Read Aloud)**
**I will change those habits that are holding me back from taking that personal risk to nurture others.**

The more we change old negative habits, the more confident we are in our interactions with others. No one human being feeling worthy of success is apt to think that mocking another person will encourage capability and individualism. Individuals who are faithful, trustworthy, and nurturing do not have to be told that mocking is not a good educational tool for adults or children. The same is true for those in business, management, or any professional role. They are not likely to think that they will draw out the best from their employees by talking about them with disrespect and hatred. Moreover, there should not be a human being in your life that is manipulating your insecurities whether it is a relative or business associate.

In the area of Paradigm Processing and Relationship Building through discourse, it is clear that while nothing is guaranteed, the best way to inspire growth is to possess it ourselves. If we wish to make a positive contribution to the confidence of an adult or child, then that feeling of worth, confidence, faithfulness, and trustworthiness (like giving to those less fortunate) begins during childhood. In other words, as adults dealing with adults, serenity inspires serenity, happiness inspires happiness, openness inspires openness, confidence inspires confidence, and when we live from the best within ourselves we are most likely to draw out the best in others.

There have been so many people that I did not know that I had an effect on until they told me what I had done in their lives just by the examples I set and my interactions with them. I remember during one of my educational symposiums, a young woman standing to tell the participants how I had changed her life. She recalled the first day that we met. It was at the University's Perspective Student Orientation. She talked about how I told the participants that they could go all the way to their Doctorate with funding paid for by financial aid, scholarships, and grants. She recalled how I used my own personal life experiences to connect with them.

After that day, she went on to earn her undergraduate, and Master Degrees and started her own businesses. This young woman was in her early thirties, had four children, and was not working before our meeting. She went on to say that she applied for scholarships, fellowships, grants, and internships just on faith. She stated that her courses and books where paid for at the undergraduate and Master's level because she took a risk and tried the methods I told her about in our advising sessions. She even received money to start her businesses, for her house, and helped her elderly father who could not work because of an illness, and payoff some of his bills.

Those initial Perspective Student Orientations were the beginning of my career as a motivational speaker. My speeches included; the risks I had taken, the courage I had to keep going when I was turned down for fellowships, grants, and scholarships, my personal experiences, successes, and my failures. The point is, if we have the courage to let others see our personal experiences, successes, and failures with excitement, we imply that excitement and experiences is a value and that they should not suppress their own experiences and excitement for life. If we let others see our enthusiasm for our aspirations, we unconditionally impart our actions on their own ability for passionate goal-seeking. If we openly and confidently contribute our own principles and inspired beliefs, we imply to others that they have a right to be proud of theirs. If we have the honesty to be who we are, we may motivate that honesty to others. Therefore, in honoring the "self", we help build relationships and paradigms with reciprocal worth. The point here is that individual uniqueness is not a negative or an enemy to relationships, but its most vital ingredient.

> *If these thoughts appear compelling to you, what do they signify in terms of your interactions with people during the next month of your life? And, the month after that?*

**(Read Aloud)**
**I will build relationships that will keep me in a positive frame of mind.**

I want to illustrate the spiritual and faithful approach to becoming victorious over the mind. We are going to talk about what we should permit and what we should not permit to happen in our lives on the road to renovating our minds.

I want to talk about the most basic strategy for conquering the mind. You must permit your experience, education, faith, and confidence to be your guide to any risk you take. I am saying that it is okay to take a risk in faith, however you should have completed any educated research, have complete trust in your experiences, and have the faith to carry out your vision. Furthermore, unless individuals are saying what you need to hear from their experiences, or their research, they are unneeded leaders of the opposition. A leader of opposition continually speaks without the experience or research to say anything about the subject, yet they want to contribute.

You cannot listen to any opposition, but allow your education, spirit, faithfulness and experience to be the confirmation for fact. Nothing else is factual, and your mind has to be focused, and clear of negativity. Your experiences and education will continually stress the timeliness of your faith regarding the risks taken to achieve your goals. Your spirit and faith in every situation you could ever face, even if you never believe it, will continually give way to the genuineness of your goals, risks, and visions. If you believe completely with your discourse, spirit, and faith, your goals will come true. I remember people calling me doctor before I had earned my doctorate. Earning my doctorate degree was put into my spirit with simple discourse – just simple statements that were intended to be a joke. At the time, I was just trying to earn my undergraduate degree. I did not believe or even thought that I wanted to go on to earn my doctorate. Nonetheless, the discourse was put into my spirit, which led to reality whether I wanted it to or not. The same is true with the negative aspects of our discourse. If you take negative discourse into your spirit, negative actions will manifest itself in the physical.

# Chapter 21

*You should never spend any time without acknowledging your spirit and faith as the base that holds you together.*

You are the consumer of your spirit, and your consumption of discourse is the food, whether you believe it or not, the food or discourse is consumed into body and spirit. Additionally, you are spontaneous in your actions, which were created by your history of consuming discourse into your spirit. With discourse, you are a new creature, and once you have true faith and you believe in your spirit the sky is the limit. You are already holistically wealthy and healthy, once you get it in your spirit through discourse. You are free from guilt because you step-out on faith, whether you ever experience it or not. A good example would be the seams of books. The seam of a book, metaphorically speaking, is your spirit and faith, and the pages of the book would be the steps you take throughout your life. You have never seen a book without seams, without the seams, the book would never stand on its own and the pages would fly away in the wind. You should never spend any time without acknowledging your spirit and faith as the base that holds you together. Without acknowledging your spirit and faith, your goals and visions of wealth and health would, "fly away in the winds of time."

Your spirit and faith is the key to keeping your mind strong when you take those educated risks needed to become successful. You may know from your experiences that the risks have minimum conse-quences. However, you have to make your spirit and faith the seams that keep your mind straight and true.

Do you want to be one of those books that stand the test of time like the Bible? Then permit your spirit and faith to be your strength even if every human being in this world says that you cannot achieve your goals. Refuse to allow any thoughts to reside in your mind that contradict your faith. With your spirit as your unconditional manual to your vision of wealth and health, you can overcome any negative thoughts whether it wants to be overcome or not. "Walk by faith and not by sight" (2 Corinthians 5:7).

**(Read Aloud)**
**I will not let any negative tendencies restrain me from taking risks that will guarantee wealth and joy in my life.**

The tendency that restrains most people is not having a course of action, and/or lack of educated research. Course of action justifies the strategy, however, your spirit and faith will encourage you to its completion. Although, the following discussion about an individual's tendency to refrain from risk – to eliminate any negative tendency, the point here is that, it would not take both faith and educated research to complete our goals. As I stated earlier, you can do it on faith alone. However, educated research would speed-up the process, or as Einstein put it, "Bend light or time." In addition, most people whorecount the experiences of others are commonly limited by the story itself, or with a common model illustrated by it, not researched the facts, which guides and tells of the methods that will help you finish with specified results.

For example, we might recount the experiences of others research-ing scholarships, grants, or fellowships. The days and nights surfing the internet, how it took time to ask the right questions, and the intriguing internet sites that wanted you to pay for the information, knowing very well that you could get the same information free via other internet sites. Most individuals, who have a tendency to hold back from achieving their goals, fit into the following two kinds of processes. Both of the processes are apparent in the preceding example of researching scholarships, grants, and fellowships.

- **The Directional Individual, which is the person who is always explaining how to do something, how to find scholarships, grants, and fellowships; but never did it themselves, and**

- **The Informational Individual, which is the person that explains how something is or was done (how the scholarships, grants, and fellowships are financed and audited), but they did it for someone else, never for him or herself.**

The Directional Individual's processes can vary from written, step-by-step instructions to a detailed plan showing how to write effective grant proposals. The informational individual's processes, on the other hand, might explain the steps of a wide variety of operations or actions or mental processes, with no "how-to-do-it" purpose at all, or how someone went about choosing what fellowship to apply for.

Most people have a tendency to hold back from taking risks because they do not have a course of action explained in uncomplicated, sequential steps. Indeed, the exact order is sometimes of greatest importance, as in an instructional manual. Nevertheless, the problem is in the mind, spirit, and the understanding of time. For those individuals who need that extra step in faith, the systematic format may need to be interrupted to reinforce the ideal with descriptions and definitions of how having faith will help people to achieve their goals. Additionally, still more of a problem, some processes defies a strict chronological treatment, because several things occur simultaneously. Still your faith and spirit stays strong to stop that fear of moving forward with your plans. Presuming too little background may quickly result in irritability, with a resulting communication block, and presuming too much will almost certainly lose him or her to panic. Like a chain, dependent on its weakest link for its strength, the entire course of action can fail because of just one unclear point that makes the rest unintelligible or trust-worthy.

**(Read Aloud)**
**By ridding myself of tendencies to hold back and taking a risk in faith, I will change my life for the best by starting every day with a smile.**

Although some people may not feel or understand the sensations of joy in your life; your smile will tell another story. By starting your day with a big smile, the apathy and despair will repress any signs of any negative consciousness, feelings, and actions from previous days.

Like a car with a blowout on a highway, out of control, negative repressive and oppressive feelings, statements, and actions can occur anywhere by anyone. On the other hand, positive statements and actions can heal any past negative statements and actions. Additionally, your ability to smile in oppressive times are an indication of your new consciousness, which may look trivial, and self-indulgent, but yet effective. A smile attracts others to you and your goals. The new you will become apparent, initially, from what people see and finally by the deeds and actions you base your life on. The first thing you should do to obtain your goals and visions of life is to always present a positive magnetic image of yourself to the public, which starts with a smile. I am not only talking about your appearance, but your actions and discourse that follows the smile – your optimism that is seen through your faith, and your brutal sensitivity to the feelings of others.

# Chapter 22

*A revolution of conscious-
ness, liberates the mindset.*

A revolution of consciousness, or liberating of the mind, is not equivalent to the present you or the past you. It is a philosophic concept,
based on an insight of what would bring you joy in the future, how to
get you to your joy, and the nature of people, and institutions that will
help you get there. It is a growth of awareness, a change of values, a
renewal of knowledge and a step toward liberation. This is about
liberating your past, because that is where awareness is most apparent,
but the physical and philosophic change is taking place in all of us,
because of the change in your paradigms or the Paradigm Shift that has
taken place in your life after you address issues of your past.

This process is liberating. The liberation of this consciousness/
mindset must be conceived as only part one of Paradigm Processing
your future. Of course, there must be an energy change as well; the
debate then becomes what comes first, energy reform, or change of
consciousness/mindset. If we assume that the latter must come first,
then the full process might be like this:

1. Change of consciousness/mindset;

2. Development of an actual way of life and culture based
on the new consciousness;

3. The rediscovery of energy and work-ethic toward your
personal goals;

4. The restructuring of values.

Eventually moderates, fundamentalists, and those who believe in your new consciousness will show you the way to the answers, and may even give you the prize of holistic wealth.

**(Read Aloud)**
**I will live everyday like it is the last day of my life.**

The reason consciousness must initiate change derives from an explanation that taking care of yourself first, is actually taking care of everyone else in time and space. In other words, when you go to school to earn your undergraduate and graduate degrees or start a business – with that degree or that business you can do better for your children, for your church, and for others in your life. Its core is the ascendancy over your mindset. A mindset that is purely for spiritual guidance, physical health, social stability, and materialistic help, and Paradigm Processing, which can allow those values to be re-energized. Through Paradigm Processing you continually build bridges and connections to positive people who know and recognize your values and zeal for life.

With a change in consciousness, without a new source of values, like building trusting, faithful, and positive relationships, would be an empty exercise. In addition, the "reformed consciousness" makeup would be worse than the old paradigm. If you do not create a value system that brings others joy, the foundation of your mindset would be broken. Real change can take place only after new values are established (i.e., political values, cultural values, economic values, personality values).

**(Read Aloud)**
**I am grateful for what I currently have and for what my future holds for me.**

That ability to be grateful is another key to a wealthy and healthy revolutionary consciousness. Being grateful is as simple as believing in your future with true faith; being grateful for all the things and people in your life now, will put a smile on your face. However, you have to openly and loudly acknowledge those things you currently have in your life, and the people you hope to materialize or meet in your future. Be grateful for your place in any political or biased system such as on your job, at your church, or in your home; being grateful for your current situation, whether you believe it is good or bad.

For example, when I was a young man my mother made us go to church every Sunday while school was in session, and every day in the summer when school was out. That was the best experience of my life, because it is still paying off. My faith and spirit has never left me, especially when I needed it the most. I believe that my success in life has always been a result of prayer and gratefulness. Back then, churches included in their services, a time for parishioners to testify and confess their sins; a time for people to share with other parishioners their stories where their prayers delivered them from their addictions, fed them when they were angry, housed them when they had no money, forgave them when they sinned, guided them through life's difficult tests, and healed them when they were sick. They would start every testimony with these words, "Giving thanks to God," and end with "Thank you Jesus." Whether they were rich or poor, they testified, showing how grateful they were.

The scope and dimensions of prayer and openly sharing your gratefulness provides encouragement for others, but also keeps you encouraged. Prayer and gratefulness is essential to a positive consciousness. It also makes a clear statement to society that you are humble and appreciative of the gift of friendship and companionship. Most people stand with people who have humanistic values and are willing to share their personal experiences, and gives thanks for their relationship. Any future you think you might have is dependent upon your ability to be grateful for your past because your past created your future. It was just a matter of time before you got to it.

**163**

Your defeats were just preludes to your billion-dollar reward, your completely healed rewards; and your finding that perfect relationship. It is similar to my experiences baking cakes. The first time I baked a cake, I burned it completely until it was charcoal black. There was nothing left of that cake, as a matter of fact I almost burned down the house. The next time I baked, the cake did not cook completely, and it was horrible. The third time I baked, the cake tasted pretty good, and the forth-time it was even better. The key is that I never gave up; my past was a prelude to a better future.

**(Read Aloud)**
**I do not care what lies on the other side, I just know what my spirit has for me in relationships.**

Any change is frightening, especially one where you are asked to change who you are. Most people change because their present situation is not working for them or in their family's best interest. Nevertheless, I do want to change your current situation; a change based on worth not on the competitiveness to get to the other side. The goal is to prepare you for your personal utopia in a competitive world. In the utopian or perfect world you are creating for yourself, there is no competition, just gratefulness, spiritual consciousness, and reward.

# Chapter 23

*I will live in victory, thinking
only victorious thoughts.*

If the core of living is having a high regard for others, information and faith, then living in victory without competition is its ultimate test. When the information we must face have to do with ourselves, being mindful can suddenly become very difficult. Here is where the challenge of true faith enters. Living in victory asks that we approach our experience with an attitude that makes the notion of approval or disapproval irrelevant: the desire to see, to know, to be aware. Now, to live in victory does not imply to be without a yearning to transform, expand, or progress. The truth is, living in victory is a prerequisite of change. If we admit the reality of what we experience and what we are, at any instance of our life we can allow ourselves to be mindful of the quality of our decisions and dealings, when we get to that point our growth is unappreciated. In other words, people love and remember those people who make positive unbiased decisions on their behalf.

Here is another simple example. Go to any large urban city in America. On a nice warm day, go to their downtown area or to any public park for an hour or two, sit, or stand across the street from any garbage can that you see. Watch how many people come to that garbage to eat. As you watch this, notice your feelings as you do so. Probably you would want to leave, want to help, or feel grateful that it is not you. If you are like most people, you will find some parts so difficult to look at for long, because they disturb you. Perhaps you see something so painful that you do not want to accept it – like a family walking to the garbage can, and you see them feeding each other from its contents.

From watching that, perhaps there is some aspect of your life that you would start to detest and that you can hardly bear to keep your eyes and mind focused on what you are looking at. Perhaps you remember throwing away food that was edible that day, and you cannot bear the thoughts and emotions those visions evoke. Therefore, the urge to avoid – to escape from those thoughts – to reject, deny, disown aspects of what you are seeing and feeling become evident.

Nonetheless, stay focused on those images, feelings, and emotions a few moments longer, and experiment with saying to yourself, "That my actions were wasteful. I will practice not to be wasteful."

**(Read Aloud)**
**Whatever is going on in my life, I accept victoriously, devotedly and completely.**

Stay focused, breathe deeply, and say this repeatedly for a minute or two, without rushing the process. Rather, allow yourself to experience fully the meaning of your words. You may find yourself complaining, "But I do not like certain things about my life – so how can I accept things victoriously, devotedly, and completely?"

Now, do you believe that you can live victoriously if you were that family feeding from the garbage can? Do you believe that your consciousness can move you forward into a future of wealth? Remember, time is relative, although you are where you are right now, does not mean you are going to be there in the next moment, minute, hour, day, week, month, or year. You need to remember that "accepting" does not necessarily mean "liking"; "accepting" does not mean we cannot imagine, or have faith in the changes that are taking place. It means experiencing, without negation or evading, that a fact is a fact; in this case, it means accepting that you have food to eat, clothes to wear, time to relax, family and friends. If you persist, if you surrender to the victory, if you surrender to being grateful (which is what "living in victory" ultimately means) you may notice that you have begun to relax a bit, and perhaps feel more comfortable with yourself, and more importantly, you may want to help your fellow man/woman.

Even though you may not like or enjoy where you are right now in life. You may not have completed that degree, you may not have passed that mathematics examination, or you may not have started that business. You may not be able to help out at the church like you wanted to, you may not be able to help your children or parents like you wanted to, your children may not have developed like you wanted them to, but you are still able to say, "Right now, that's me, that's my life and I am victorious. Moreover, I do not deny that fact. I accept it with a feeling of victory."

Admitting that, says that you value reality, and at the same time you value your spirit and faith. Within a very short period of time, you will begin to experience the relationship between living in victory, living grateful, and living in reality. Soon you will discover that you are becoming mentally balanced with yourself. You will begin to feel like there is nothing you cannot achieve, that you cannot accomplish, or change. If there were aspects of yourself that you did not like before, or was not within your control, you will be more motivated to make the necessary changes once you have accepted the facts, as they are now.

Our feeling of victory is not led by our history, as some people naively believe. Our feeling of victory comes from our willingness to see and accept ourselves as we are, and the consequences of risks we take in faith.

Suppose you are about to present your research to a group of professors from universities all over the country and you are terrified. You are tormented by your fear. You try to fight it the way most people do: by tensing your body, constricting your breathing, and telling yourself, "Don't be afraid." This strategy does not work. In fact, the feeling of torment gets worse and worse. Your body is now sending your brain the signals of an emergency alert, the signals of danger, to which you typically respond by saying to yourself, "I can do this, I did enough research, I put together a discussion that would prove my research," and with dread, frustration and self-criticism, you tell yourself, "I cannot do this." You are at war with yourself, because you do not know what else to do. No one has ever taught you, and you have never learned, that an alternative strategy exists that is far more helpful, the strategy of living in victory by true faith.

In this strategy, you do not fight the feelings of distress; rather, you breathe into it, and accept it. You stop telling yourself, "I can't do it," perhaps you tell yourself, "I am afraid, but how can I do it?" Then you take a long, slow, deep breath, and reflect on the victory. Even though this is difficult at first and may remain difficult for some time, you reflect and you watch your fear become a witness to the victory, without identifying with the fear, without allowing the fear to define you, continue to reflect on the victory.

**(Read Aloud)**
**If I am afraid, but that is no reason to not live in the victory – to continue to see the victory.**

You may even want to have open discourse with your fear. Allowing your fears to reveal the most horrible and conceivable thing that could happen. You do this so that your fears can be faced and accepted with the reality of the situation. I know that this approach cultivates more tormenting fantasies. When you reflect on the victory, you will be grateful for the opportunity. Your fear may not always disappear – sometimes it will, sometimes it will only diminish in its effectiveness on your life, but you have to find ways to overcome this to live victoriously.

**(Read Aloud)**
**I am a stronger person now that I understand that my spirit and faith will take me beneath my present into a perfect future.**

We are always stronger when we do not try to fight the truth. Many more people will never experience the power of faith. We cannot make our feelings of dread go away by shrinking the truth about our addictions, or fighting ourselves for being unfaithful or not willing to take a risk to see our visions through to the end. We surely cannot make that feeling of faithlessness go away indulging in self-criticism. However, we must open-up to our experiences of victory, stay faithful, remember that our spirit is larger than any one emotion, and that we can achieve great things.

If a person is afraid, it is usually pointless to tell him or her to "relax." The person does not know how to translate that advice into behavior. However, if you talk of imagining all of the victorious things that he or she had accomplished prior to this event, it gives them something tangible to actualize. You want them to remember what it felt like to be victorious, how many times they were victorious, and what it felt like to fight in faith for the victory.

Nevertheless, it is important that we allow the faithlessness in, even welcome faithlessness, making friends with it – or at least watch it without identifying with it and then finally work hard/smartly to turn that faithlessness into victory.

**(Read Aloud)**
**I am feeling faithlessness, and I can accept that fact, but I am more than my faithlessness. I am faithful, and willing to work hard for my victory.**

This is a very powerful device for handling faithlessness (or any other unwanted feelings). These are actions you can learn from, rehearse in imagination, and practice when situations arise when you need your faith. The practice I am describing is appropriate for virtually any feelings of dread. It is useful when you are dealing with a poorly behaved child, a cheating wife or husband, a racist or sexist supervisor, or preparing to defend a murderer, when having to tell someone painful information, when struggling with rejection or abandonment.

When you learn to accept the fact that there will be times when you will be faithless, you cease making it a devastating event. Then it ceases to be your master, yet the fact that you thought about your faith, and how it can make the difference between trying and not trying at all is a revolution of your consciousness. You are no longer tormented by what could happen and what is going to happen. You feel more successful. You feel more in control of your life. Your self-confidence and your self-respect will rise.

**(Read Aloud)**
**I will allow my spirit and discourse with others to be a buffer between reality and faith.**

After keynoting a seminar, I had the pleasure of meeting a young man who I thought had complete faith in his spirit and in his wife. He attended church with his kids regularly. At first, we talked about him completing his education. We talked about ways to fund his education and the courses he should take to achieve his goals. As time passed, the discussions got more personal. Eventually, he started to talk about his pending divorce. He told me how he worked, and took care of his children while his wife was earning her Doctorate degree. He informed me that right after she completed her degree, she filed for divorce. He told me that after 12 years of marriage, he was now living in his mother's basement, while his wife was working to take his children and home from him.

He told me how he took his children to church every Sunday for service, and Wednesday for Bible study. One day after court, he came to see me crying and confused. Apparently, his wife had hired a lawyer and because he had faith, he decided to defend himself. He stated that he had gone to see his clergy and a marriage counselor prior to seeing me. The marriage counselor, clergy, and I told him the same thing, "Get a lawyer." He refused, and at the next court hearing, while he was crying in his seat, the judge was about to give everything to his wife, when the judge said, "Sir, you really need a lawyer and I am going to give you one week to get one." At that point, he reflected on what the clergy told him, "Have faith in God who will send you a lawyer that will represent you and your children who need their father in their lives."

After court, the judge gave him some numbers to call and before the day was over, he had one of the best divorce attorneys in the city, free of charge. The point is that he had faith. He not only was awarded the time to see his children regularly, and because she received a new position and raise, he was awarded enough alimony to pay rent in a new apartment.

I will never forget his ability to keep his faith, and his ability to have faith in the discourse of others. Discourse is always used to nudge your spirit, it is the water when you are thirsty, or the food when you are hungry. Take a few minutes to contemplate some feelings or emotions of yours that is not easy for you to face i.e., faithlessness, insecurity, pain, envy, rage, sorrow, humiliation, dread, or fear. When you differentiate the feeling, see if you can focus on it clearly, maybe by thinking about what induced it. Then breathe into the feeling, as if opening your body to it. Imagine what it would feel like not to resist this feeling but to accept it fully. Explore that experience. Take your time. Practice saying to yourself, *"I am now feeling such and such (whatever the feeling is) and I accept it fully."*

At first, this may be difficult. You may find that you feel some faithlessness. However, you need to keep on going; talk to your spirit, tell yourself that you are faithful. Remind yourself of the reality of the sit-

**171**

uation, ("A fact is a fact, that which is, is, if the feeling exists, it exists.") keep contemplating the feeling. Think of allowing the feeling to be there, rather than trying to wish or will it out of existence. You may find it useful, as I have, to tell yourself, *"I am now exploring the world of fear or pain or envy, confusion or faithlessness and I am okay with it."* In so doing, you will be exploring how it feels to live in victory.

I remember sitting in the waiting area prior to my interview with the Admissions Committee for admissions to my Doctorate program. There were some people ahead of me, which gave me a lot of time to feel a maximum amount of fear, pain, and faithlessness. In response to the shock of going before the committee members, and the pain of the first question, I stopped breathing and contracted my whole body, as if to hold off an invading army. Nonetheless, I was tense which made it difficult to make sense of my thoughts. As I thought about what questions might be asked, I began to think of all of the victories I had accomplished in my life. I began to think of the faith I had in my spirit. I began to have discourse with myself. I said aloud, "I am so grateful for victory."

As I entered the room, I took a deep breath, drawing energy from within. I realized that I was living in the victory of my life. I accepted my reality and any feelings of faithlessness rather than treat it as an adversary. This strategy is very familiar, of course, to athletes and dancers, whose work requires them to "ride with" pain rather than convulse against it. It is similar to Lamaze breathing exercises that are taught to pregnant women for controlling and easing pain, anxiety, and body reactions that embody precisely the principle we are considering here.

**(Read Aloud)**
**I will add to the strength of my faith foundation by admitting I feel the way I feel.**

After we accept the fact that our actions are our actions, there is still the issue of evaluation in a way that nurtures rather than undermine our faith and our paradigm. Anything that we have the likelihood of feeling, we have the likelihood of renouncing, either immediately or later, in memory. Anything that does not fit our official perception or our official belief system, or that evokes anxiety for any reason whatsoever, we can reject. For example, I can decline to recognize my sensuality and I can decline to recognize my spirituality. I can refuse to acknowledge my grief and I can refuse to acknowledge my joy. I can repress my faith, I can repress the memory of actions I am ashamed of and I can repress the memory of actions I am proud of. The problem of self-repression is by no means confined to the "negatives."

We can be as terrified of our assets as we are of our shortcomings. We can be terrified by our genius, ambition, excitement, faith, or beauty as of our emptiness, passivity, depression, unattractiveness, or faithlessness. It is our responsibility to accept these things, because if you do not, it would guarantee a problem in our relationships with others. Our responsibility is to take care of ourselves, and maintain a positive productive paradigm with others.

# Chapter 24

*I will have vigor for life.*

Our vigor for life makes us feel enthusiastic, adventurous, confident, spiritual, and energetic. On-the-other-hand, our vigor for life, for our goals and vision, or virtues can make us feel alone, alienated, cut-off from those who lack faith, lack the understanding of Paradigm Processing their future, where you become a target for envy and hostility. Additionally, vigor for life overcomes any of our desire to belong, and can overcome any desire to actualize our highest potential, our highest goals, or our risk taking in faith. It may take great courage to be willing to admit, even in the privacy of our own minds that, "I can do things others do not seem able to do." Or, "I am more intelligent than anyone else in my family." Or, "I am unusually good-looking." Or, "I want more out of life than the people around me." Or, "I see farther and more clearly than the average person." I have special gifts.

I recall a young woman who came to see me for advisement many years ago. She was around thirty-seven years old, she had the face of a person who had seen and experienced many things, good and bad. She was an accountant without an undergraduate degree. She talked about how she had been working at her company for years and could not move up in the company or get a raise because she did not have a degree. She spent 11 years at that company and wanted to change her life for the better, or at least earn her degree and go on to become a CPA (Certified Public Accountant). She stated that she could perform any duty that any accountant at her company could perform. She went on to say that she had seen many people fired because they thought that they knew more than the accountants with degrees. She stated that at meetings she would sit quietly whispering to herself, "Please, God, if she asks me a question, please do not let me know the answer." I asked, "Why?" She answered, "Because they hate you if you know too much. They hate you if you are too smart." One day before the semester began, when we were discussing her schedule, she became very angry with me. She felt really badly about the previous semester, how she had disconnected from her family. When she could not articulate her reasons, I invited her to explain. Like most adult students, she missed family events, church, and holiday get-togethers. I asked her did she have faith in the things she was doing for herself and her family. This caused her to think about why she had become so resentful. "The good thing about you, Dr. Martin, is that you believe everything has to be done by faith, and you have confidence in the human spirit. You refuse to see people as lost or confused. You make people feel good about themselves, because some people hate the truth or just will not accept it. You make people feel like there is hope regardless of the situation." She went on, "You make me believe in myself. I actually believe that I can go on to earn my license." I have not heard from that young lady in years, but the last I heard of her, she was earning her MBA.

Sometimes the path to living in victory, living in joy, and living with true faithfulness comes from the person you least expect. Any person can change their paradigm, change their lens, or change how they feel about their spirit or soul. We cannot fully know in advance when someone is going to help us through an event or an experience that will make us stronger in our journey. The more we are willing to experience and control the many diverse viewpoints of who we are, the richer our personal paradigm, the greater our physical, emotional, and social resources, the more appropriate we will feel about the challenges and opportunities of life. Additionally, it is more likely that we will find, or create a Paradigm Shift existence that meets our individual needs.

An attitude of Paradigm Processing your future of wealth and joy by living in victory, believing in true faith, awakens a person's drive to have positive productive discourse. This attitude can inspire a person to face whatever he or she dreads without collapsing into self-pity, not accepting his or her value as a person, or surrendering the will to live in victory, in acceptance of the spirit. Thus, a person might be unhappy about experiencing faithlessness yet accept it along with the self-doubts and feelings of guilt.

Sometimes people confuse the whole subject of living in victory and faith by believing and making note that everyone has faith in spite of anything he or she does or fails to do. This is entirely ridiculous. They are confusing faith with living in victory, which necessarily depends on certain abilities, with such an ability to reflect; throughout life from victory to victory, failure to failure, each victory and failure making your faith stronger.

Most of the adult students that I advise and counsel have had bad experiences believing that they can do anything, or achieve anything starting with the victory first, especially, testing. Here is a simple sentence-completion exercise that I ask them to do to address the issue of living in victory, and living in acceptance. Now, they must answer the questions right there in front of you, rapidly, without any time to really go into deep thought about the answers. They must rapidly say or write whatever comes to their minds, and that is what you want to read or hear. Take a notebook or just ask the questions aloud, whatever would work best for you at that moment, and ask the following known psychological questions:

- **Sometimes I dislike myself when I-**
- **I do not like me because-**

- I like me because-
- I do not like when I-
- I like myself most when I-
- My mother made me feel like a-
- My father made me feel like a-
- When I feel people dislike me it is because I-
- When I am feeling good about me, I-
- The scary thing about taking a risk is that-
- When I feel dread, my spirit is at its-
- If I allow myself to experience the joy of being victorious, I would...

Now that you took the time to take part in this exercise, you have caused your mindset and/or paradigm to react to those feelings of faithlessness, worries, dread, fears, and guilt, because now you have an idea where those thoughts are coming from. However, the breakthrough may not be acknowledged at first, but your conscious will hold on to the discovery. You might want to forget and refuse to accept it, to confront the responsibility of living in faith, living in victory, and living in expectancy without fear of risk or guilt.

Nevertheless, when you do not live in faith, expecting victory, willing to take that risk that will bring joy to your life, the deepest and most primal quantity of your existence will be apt to turn against you. The point is, if we do not love ourselves enough, we are offending our spirit, and in-effect weakening our future, while forgetting our past victories. For example, if I do not have the faithfulness to stand by my wife, my wife feels let down by me. By this token, if I do not have the faithfulness to stand by myself (which means the courage to know that I like myself and to embrace the responsibility of doing so), then I, too, feel let down, even though I may be incapable of explaining my feelings of faithlessness and dread.

**(Read Aloud)**
**I do not choose to settle for less than what is possible for my life. I choose to make the best of my life and I will. I cannot settle for less than what is possible.**

You may accept your attributes, thoughts, feelings, or actions, while denying or disowning other areas of your life. Make a list of six things that you feel weakens your faith in yourself. Remember that acknowledging facts does not mean understanding or agreeing with them. Then, write six to ten resolutions where you can take a risk in faith. Maybe it is at that moment that it will become clearer to you that taking a risk in faith is truly living in victory. Now, I want you to take the next several days entrusting your spirit and faith by living in victory. If you want to live in complete victory, openly and freely, give back your time, your faithful strength, and your talents. From giving in faith you will receive what the wealthiest people in the world already know.

For example, there is a tremendous spiritual lesson to be learned when the world's two richest people give away so much of their wealth to help others in need. In 2000, the world's richest person, Microsoft co-founder Bill Gates, launched the Gates Foundation to focus on strengthening education, reducing poverty and improving public health, with a special emphasis on HIV, malaria and tuberculosis. (Gates, B., Gates, M., 2009).

Mr. Gates has since given $29 billion of his own assets to charities, including $23 billion to the Gates Foundation, making it the world's largest philanthropic organization. Gates also recently announced that he would be ending his full-time role at Microsoft in 2008 so that the majority of his time could be focused on the foundation.

Gates' friend of 15 years and the second-richest person in the world, Warren Buffett, recently announced that he will be contributing roughly $31 billion to the Gates Foundation. Buffett will be joining the

Gates Foundation board, helping to ensure that the resources are wisely stewarded and that as many people as possible are helped (Driscoll, 2006).

# Chapter 25

*With a loving spirit comes great wealth.*

From a spiritual perspective, Bill and Melinda Gates' generosity illustrates an important Biblical truth. Sadly, wealth is often viewed through the erroneous lens of either the prosperity or poverty theology. In the prosperity theology, God loves rich people more than he loves poor people, as evidenced by his blessing. In the poverty theology, God loves poor people more than he loves rich people, who are vilified as greedy thieves. The problem with both of these theologies is that they make money the issue. The real issue is not money, but righteousness. There are not two kinds of people – rich and poor – but four kinds of people: the righteous rich, the unrighteous rich, the righteous poor, and the unrighteous poor.

The righteous rich became rich because God blessed them; they worked hard, invested wisely, and did not obtain wealth through sin like stealing or taking advantage of others. Such people spend their money righteously, generously sharing their abundance with those in need. I do not know the religious convictions of Gates or Buffett, but their generosity is an example of rich people acting in a righteous manner. The unrighteous rich are people who obtain wealth through immoral means such as stealing, extorting, selling harmful addictive drugs, and/or false profiteering. They do little if anything to help people in need. The righteous poor are people who work hard for the little they have, spend it to survive, give to their church, and share a meager amount with others in need. The unrighteous poor are people with little or no money because they are lazy or spend foolishly. They do not give to God or others. When the issue of money is framed as rich and poor instead of righteous and unrighteous, we are allowing politics and economics rather than spiritual wisdom to dominate our thinking. The generosity of Gates and Buffett is an opportunity for each of us to evaluate whether we are acting righteously with the little or great wealth we have.

**(Read Aloud)**
**I understand that my spirit will not give me more if I am not trusted to give more.**

Anyone of normal intelligence who possesses a fair portion of self-control can give to those less fortunate. There is only one way to improve your life, your faith, and your health and that is to give back in faith. Let me make it clear, when I discuss your spirit, I am referring to your higher power; the power that keeps you balanced in the spirit. Our spirit tells us who is faithful, trustworthy, and delivered in the spirit. Those individuals delivered in the spirit recognize the marvelous power of living in victory, believing in the spirit, and faith. They know the promise of the spirit, and those who are faithful in the spirit, and believing in the spirit shall have discourse with others like them. They know that in the spirit, wealth will multiply, health will return, and joy will follow them throughout their time on this planet. More importantly, it should not be used for the benefit of selfish goods, but for the benefit of humanity, and the spirit. Moreover, we should divide our "inheritance" among our family in spirit and faith. Let your spirit be your guide. I remember trying to rent a townhouse in the Chicago-land area. At that time, it was very difficult to find good renters – renters that paid their rent on time, did not destroy your property, respect your wishes as the owner of the property. I remember talking to so many potential renters who implicitly or explicitly, let me know that they were going to be a bad renter. Here are a few indicators: Many of them drove up to the house smoking or they came to the interview with their dog. They said things like: I am $49,000 in debt, or the place I am renting right now, I stopped paying rent six months ago, or I own property already, I just want to rent in this area.

My spirit always interposed, to guide me in the right direction. I just had to open myself up to receive the message. Understanding how your spirit works will work for the advancement of your temporal affairs; but your spiritual truths have to take hold of your mind and heart. The giving of yourself, and your time in faith is the absorbing theme of spirituality. We see it all over the world, the wealthy and poor giving whatever fortune they have in faith to a person, a cause, or church.

Simply put, you have always heard from your spirit, in your conscious, you have always seen yourself wealthy, healthy, and/or contributing to society and humanity. Your spirit has always been pleading with you to step out on faith, to become an heir of your birthright. However, your faith cannot be incorruptible by money, land, alcohol, or drugs. It must be a faith that will never fade away – that is always open to bettering yourself and others in faith.

Now there are opportunities for you to have discourse with your spirit, to express your desires in your uppermost heart. The secret is to keep your faith, be grateful for the gifts you have right now and put your spirit first. Never use the gifts of your spirit as a means of worldly gain, but as a means to help others.

All of us will eventually die in the physical. No one lives forever in the physical, however, some of us will live forever in the hearts, minds, and souls of others by the deeds they did prior to death in the physical. A good example of this would be Dr. Martin Luther King Jr. – King truly worked for the social good. He never let greed turn his faith, or his spirit, from his willingness to serve society, and the human good. He never diverted from the mission of his spirit, the strength of his faith.

**182**

King used discourse with his spirit to guide him, he listened to his spirit, and he was guided by his spirit to say the right thing and to motivate people to do the right thing – his words, his legacy, will live on forever.

In the spirit, to magnetize what you need, and what you want out of life, tell people about the goodness of faith in the spirit, and about your ability to live in victory. Tell them that they can give back by volunteering at the hospital, volunteering at the local elderly home, local church, or by mentoring, or coaching children at their local park district. In other words, give freely and receive freely.

Giving to others is a spiritual connection; it makes you a blessing to humanity. If you have never given to another person who was less fortunate than you were – you have never truly lived in connection with your spirit. Giving feels good, and it renews your spirit and faith. Your spirit alone gives the new heart of love from the selfish heart of self-interest. Your spirit alone gives new wealth from the lack of wealth. Your spirit alone can give holistic health from poor health. Just loudly and proudly, let people and your higher power know about your grate-fulness and your faith in the spirit. Tell them of your victories, and re-ceive by the grace of your spirit, your faith, and your hope for them. Then such results will be manifested, in the blessing and uplifting of humanity.

Look out for those troubled people that will try to manifest their spirit in connection with your spirit for materialist greed. When you come across those individuals, just have discourse with them about how there is enough for everyone. So much that they will not have enough room to hold it all. However, you cannot hold on to your riches for self-ish reasons, and you must give thanks to your spirit, and your faith. If you gain your wealth for yourself, and is not rich in the spirit you will surely lose it all, because you have more faith in the wealth than you have in the spirit. The spirit is where your wealth will originate. You must Paradigm Process your consciousness to always give thanks to your spirit and be grateful for your past, present, and future.

We all have to be grateful for what we have, and thank our spirit from whom all blessings come. What a blessing for all of those who have been faithful to their spirit, asking their spirit for help, and helping others, although they had little to nothing themselves. All they have to do is find the many places in which to bestow their "wealth" in the name of faith.

As men and women, living in victory, we do not plan for ourselves; we plan for giving, for sharing, for the faithfulness of our spirit. Within our spirit, we can see everything that is in front of us, just open-up and listen. We regard ourselves as favored above other men and women, but take no credit for our victory, it comes from our spirit, and we honor people in the physical and in the spiritual. For as men and women of the spirit, living in faith and victory openly praise our spirit who is willing to receive a life of victory. Remember, Martin Luther King Jr. will live forever in the hearts and souls of men and women because of the things he accomplished and the sacrifice he made for others. Your ability to live in victory, your faith in the spirit to sacrifice your old paradigm for the good of others will guarantee you and your family wealth for generations.

My final wish for you is to:

- Fight the good fight of faith,

- Fearlessly make known your goals,

- Strengthen your physical and emotional power, so that you may have great endurance and patience,

- Generously give of yourself,

- Cultivate your ability to show true humility towards all,

- Be strong and courageous in your character and actions,

- Show proper respect for everyone,

- Show mercy and compassion, and act justly in all that you do,

- Allow your spirit to guide you in faith, and in all circumstances create a paradigm of righteousness,

- Allow the tranquility of knowing that the fact that you live in victory rules in your heart,

- Never allow yourself to grow in faithlessness, but strive for the mastery of the spiritual life,

- Allow your body to be the instrument of righteousness, and your wealth to be a bridge connecting you with the less fortunate,

- Examine your paradigm on a regular basis, making sure you are walking in line with the spirit, in faithfulness, righteousness, and gratefulness.

Thank you. Now go start living!!!!

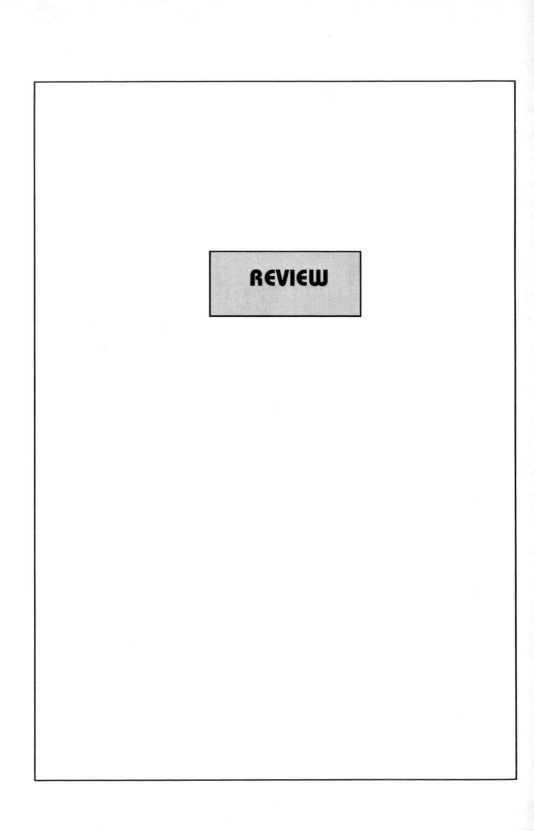

REVIEW

## A Paradigm of Proactive Thinking in Faith

- Can you take a risk on you?
- Can you take control of your fears?
- Can you always remember your vision of success?
- Do you want to live the best life now?
- Can you do what it takes to be happy, and joyful?

## Loyalty

- Loyalty: success will never come unless you are loyal to your visions.
- How? It's not hard, just do what you love.

## Education

- Education: You must educate yourself formally or informally to assure your success.
- How? School or learn by experience.

## Reflect and Review

- Reflect on those opportunities past, present, and in the future.
- Daily, look at every opportunity as one that advances your goals and dreams.

## Praise Daily

- List the things you can praise about on a daily basis.

| | |
|---|---|
| **1.** | |
| **2.** | |
| **3.** | |
| **4.** | |

- List four things that would change the paradigm you currently have, or present to others. What paradigm shift do you want to occur now? What do you admire in others that you do not see in yourself?

| | |
|---|---|
| **1.** | |
| **2.** | |
| **3.** | |
| **4.** | |

## Develop the paradigm that would bring you closer to your vision

*Negative Discourse, Negative Relationships*

- You cannot be successful if you have negative discourse, and negative relationships. Having negative discourse and negative relationships allows you to live out negative outcome, whether than living in victory.

## Create Positive Statements, and then ask yourself, do you live by these statements?

| | |
|---|---|
| **1.** | |
| **2.** | |
| **3.** | |
| **4.** | |

- What words of wisdom and faith has given meaning to your life?

| | |
|---|---|
| **1.** | |
| **2.** | |
| **3.** | |
| **4.** | |

- What are some of the things you believed you would never do, that you are doing now?

| | |
|---|---|
| **1.** | |
| **2.** | |
| **3.** | |
| **4.** | |

- What is it that you would do with your life without being compensated?

| | |
|---|---|
| **1.** | |
| **2.** | |
| **3.** | |
| **4.** | |

## Create Vision/Set Goals

It does no good to simply set goals unless you devote some thought to creating truly meaningful goals. Go over the following questions when considering how your vision is going to be focused.

- What do you want to accomplish in your life?

| | |
|---|---|
| **1.** | |
| **2.** | |
| **3.** | |
| **4.** | |

- What do you want to leave behind as your legacy?

| | |
|---|---|
| **1.** | |
| **2.** | |
| **3.** | |
| **4.** | |

- What ground rules are your goals built upon? What values, beliefs, or principles matter most to you?

| | |
|---|---|
| **1.** | |
| **2.** | |
| **3.** | |
| **4.** | |

- Why do you want to achieve your goals? Will society benefit? Will those around you benefit? Is it linked to things you believe in? How?

**1.** Read and learn as much about those goals as possible.

**2.** Find role models whose vision/goals you could study either up close or from afar.

**3.** Find one or more coaches/mentors willing to give you advice and encouragement.

**4.** Make strategic alliances with other individuals, businesses, consultants, and corporations in order to provide a broad range of services. How?

**1.** Write a mission statement.

|  |
|  |
|  |

**2.** Build a strong reciprocal learning network of contacts tied together through personal relationships.

| **1.** |  |
|---|---|
| **2.** |  |
| **3.** |  |
| **4.** |  |

**Develop loving and loyal relationships as you go**

- Think of people who have come into your life because they could see what you see for yourself. These people might be relatives or friends of the family, faculty, and/or coaches, anybody who has stepped in and helped you refine your vision for your life. This could be people sitting in the room today.

| | |
|---|---|
| **1.** | |
| **2.** | |
| **3.** | |
| **4.** | |

- Make a list of four potential mentors who can help guide you to your vision. Make definite and specific plans for contacting these potential mentors and for seeking their guidance.

| | |
|---|---|
| **1.** | |
| **2.** | |
| **3.** | |
| **4.** | |

**Be consistent in your relationships with courage and conviction.**

When you build a relationship, you have to keep your actions and reactions consistent.

**Develop a character-building journey of your actions and reactions.**

- What can you do that will allow you to feel good and others to feel good around you?

| 1. |
|----|
| 2. |
| 3. |
| 4. |

- A better life does not necessarily mean more money or a bigger house, or vacations. A joyful, faithful, and victorous life can simply mean a life with meaning; a rewarding life and a life that contributes to the common good. A life that nurtures goodness in others.

## Develop steps that will help you to get to where you need to be

- If you need help ask a friend, a teacher, a counselor, a role model or a mentor, or one of your family members to help you brainstorm about actions you might take to move you toward your goals.

| 1. |
|----|
| 2. |
| 3. |
| 4. |

- Write down nineteen things you can do that would move you closer to your goals for your education, personal life, your career, or your involvement in the community.

| | |
|---|---|
| **1.** | |
| **2.** | |
| **3.** | |
| **4.** | |
| **5.** | |
| **6.** | |
| **7.** | |
| **8.** | |
| **9.** | |
| **10.** | |
| **11.** | |
| **12.** | |
| **13.** | |
| **14.** | |
| **15.** | |
| **16.** | |
| **17.** | |
| **18.** | |
| **19.** | |

- Now, identify four of the nineteen items that are likely to have the greatest influence on moving you toward your goal.

| 1. |
|---|
| 2. |
| 3. |
| 4. |

- My goal is:

| 1. |
|---|
| 2. |
| 3. |
| 4. |

- The steps I could take to move me toward those goals are:

| 1. |
|---|
| 2. |
| 3. |
| 4. |

- Two activities I could undertake to take those steps are:

|  |
|  |

## Tearing down the walls

When putting together your weekly activity list, resist the typical inclination to think of personal, work, and family activities as separate.

- **Activity 1: Date**      **Day of the Week**      **Time**

- **Activity 2: Date**      **Day of the Week**      **Time**

- **Activity 3: Date**      **Day of the Week**      **Time**

- **Activity 4: Date**      **Day of the Week**      **Time**

- **Activity 5: Date**      **Day of the Week**      **Time**

- **Activity 6: Date**      **Day of the Week**      **Time**

- **Activity 7: Date**      **Day of the Week**      **Time**

## Listen with Love

- Be open to new ideas.
- Allow yourself to love the journey.
- Everyday, praise and give thanks for a new opportunity to get closer to your vision.

## Master your emotions
  – Increase your self-awareness so that you are in control of emotions and feelings that may have held you back in the past.
  – Feel good about your life everyday.
  – Develop triggers that would change your emotions from the negative to the positive.

| 1. |
|---|

## Determination Overcomes Adversity
- Write down some things you can do to make sure that as you pursue your goals and your vision, you also take care of your body and your health.

- To ensure my physical health I will:

| 1. |
|---|
| 2. |
| 3. |
| 4. |

- To ensure my social health I will:

| 1. |
|---|
| 2. |
| 3. |
| 4. |

- To ensure my mental health I will:

| | |
|---|---|
| **1.** | |
| **2.** | |
| **3.** | |
| **4.** | |

- To ensure my spiritual health I will:

| | |
|---|---|
| **1.** | |
| **2.** | |
| **3.** | |
| **4.** | |

## Keeping both eyes on the prize:

– Each of us has the will, and the power of the imagination to tap into when we formulate our plans for acting upon our goals and pursuing a vision.

– Let your conscience be your guide

– Tap into your willpower

– Be open to new opportunities

**Be honest** - *when you are honest with people even when you fail, you at least maintain your credibility over-time.*

**Do the work that is required** - *you know in your heart what you need to do to realize your goals.*

**Maintain a positive attitude** - *being positive begins with eliminating the negative.*

**Take the time to think things through** - *those who take time to think and plan their lives are the ones who get the greatest benefit.*

**Pause** – *Take a minute to think about your journey and then begin in faith.*

## Be spiritual and faithful in your endeavors

- You have to step-out on faith, take educated risks, whether that means trying a new job, leaving an unhealthly relationship, or offering yourself as a candidate for a community leadership position.

- Taking care of business with courage and conviction: *a system for taking care of number one in order to take care of others.*
    - Take pleasure in being in control of your own life.
    - Feel free to express your uniqueness and your own needs.
    - Do not feel guilty about saying "no," when "no" is the right thing to do.
    - Let people know your visions loudly and proudly.

## Be a faithful steward?
   – What can you do in faith today that would change your paradigm of life?

1.

- What is the one thing you fear the most about stepping out on faith?

| 1. |
|---|

- What one habit holds you back from being a faithful steward?

| 1. |
|---|

- How would this faithful leap change your life?

| 1. |
|---|
| 2. |
| 3. |
| 4. |

- What lies on the other side? If you step-out on faith, where will it put you in the victory progression?

| 1. |
|---|

- Will it add to the paradigm you are creating for yourself, which consists of your relationships, your career, and your community? _____
- Alternatively, will it weaken the positive aspects of your paradigm? _____

• Write down the potential benefits of being a faithful steward:

| | |
|---|---|
| **1.** | |
| **2.** | |
| **3.** | |
| **4.** | |

• Write down the potential problems (downside) of this faithful leap:

| | |
|---|---|
| **1.** | |
| **2.** | |
| **3.** | |
| **4.** | |

• Now weigh the potential benefits against the downside and ask yourself, "Will this move me closer to fulfilling my vision for my life, or could it potentially set me back?"

| | |
|---|---|
| **1.** | |
| **2.** | |
| **3.** | |
| **4.** | |

• **Look before you leap**
    – The fear that is holding me back from pursuing a better life is:

| | |
|---|---|
| **1.** | |
| **2.** | |
| **3.** | |
| **4.** | |

    – To overcome it, I will:

| | |
|---|---|
| **1.** | |
| **2.** | |
| **3.** | |
| **4.** | |

## Everyday guide and ready your paradigm for success

- Build on your power of positivity
    - Dealing well with negative circumstances is important, but creating and managing your responses to negative circumstances is probably an even greater part of the victory progression.

- Write down something that you want to change to better your life:
    - The changes I would like to make are:

| | |
|---|---|
| **1.** | |
| **2.** | |
| **3.** | |
| **4.** | |

• What has stopped you from making this change in the past?

| | |
|---|---|
| **1.** | |
| **2.** | |
| **3.** | |
| **4.** | |

• What fears and emotions can you anticipate when making this change?

| | |
|---|---|
| **1.** | |
| **2.** | |
| **3.** | |
| **4.** | |

• What criticisms from within and from others will accompany this change?

| | |
|---|---|
| **1.** | |
| **2.** | |
| **3.** | |
| **4.** | |

• How will making this change make your life better?

| | |
|---|---|
| **1.** | |
| **2.** | |
| **3.** | |
| **4.** | |

• What other changes, positive or negative, will accompany this one?

• Negative changes:

| | |
|---|---|
| **1.** | |
| **2.** | |
| **3.** | |
| **4.** | |

• Positive changes:

| | |
|---|---|
| **1.** | |
| **2.** | |
| **3.** | |
| **4.** | |

• Will it be worthwhile to make this change in your life? _____

• What steps do you have to go through to bring about this change? _____

## Build a team that is faithful and trustworthy

- Be consistent
    - Make a list of the people who fit your mission:

| | |
|---|---|
| **1.** | |
| **2.** | |
| **3.** | |
| **4.** | |

## Move on your vision with research

- Six Small Steps for Getting Pass Procrastination
    - Begin NOW!!!!
    - Slam the door on critics
    - Relax
    - Bring in a coach
    - Enjoy each moment of the journey
    - Do not demand perfection

## GET READY

- Develop educated alternative solutions or courses of actions.

| | |
|---|---|
| **1.** | |
| **2.** | |
| **3.** | |
| **4.** | |

- Will there be a "win/win" outcome for everyone involved?
    - Which alternative is best?

| | |
|---|---|
| **1.** | |
| **2.** | |
| **3.** | |
| **4.** | |

    – Can the best alternative meet the essential requirements? _____

- Write them down:

| | |
|---|---|
| **1.** | |
| **2.** | |
| **3.** | |
| **4.** | |

- What will the effect be on your personal relationships, your career, your place in the community, and your short and long-term values?

| | |
|---|---|
| **1.** | |
| **2.** | |
| **3.** | |
| **4.** | |

- Is it negative or positive in terms of your overall paradigm? _____
- Is it also a "win/win" situation for friends and family?

_____

**Be prepare for the naysayers**
– It is important to prepare yourself for conflict and to always keep in mind your vision with courage and conviction. Very little is accomplished without at least some sacrifices and/or temporary setbacks. You may have to go deep into your reserves of patience and resilience to manage the change. Keep in mind that you made the decision carefully and thoughtfully and that ultimately it should move you closer to your dreams and goals.

**Commit to the new paradigm you are creating for yourself**
> – Control your emotions and feelings of dread and fear.

- Write down what you are going to commit to today.

| | |
|---|---|
| **1.** | |
| **2.** | |
| **3.** | |
| **4.** | |

• Write down any commitments you have made that you have not honored.

| | |
|---|---|
| 1. | |
| 2. | |
| 3. | |
| 4. | |

• In the next week, I commit to three actions that will move me closer to my vision.

| | |
|---|---|
| 1. | |
| 2. | |
| 3. | |
| 4. | |

Commit to reflection, reciprocal learning, research, and your responsibility to society.

# References

Adult Education Quarterly, *A journal of research and theory,* (1997). Winter Vol 47, n2, 8,108-116.

Anderson, D.R., Sweeney, D.J., & Williams, T.A. (1996). *Statistics for business and economics* Chattanooga, TN: The University of Tennessee at Chattanooga, 150.

Barnes, B. (1982) *T. S. Kuhn and social science,* New York, NY: Columbia University Press, 24, 11-35.

Beauboeuf-Lafontant, T. & Smith, D.A. (Eds.). (1996). *Facing racism in education* (2nd ed.). Cambridge, MA: Harvard Educational Review.

Bittel, R. L. (1984). *Leadership the key to management success,* New York, NY: Franklin Watts, 156.

Born, M. (1967). *Einstein's theory of relativity,* New York, NY: Dover Publications, Inc., 31, 56-87.

Covey, S. R. (1989). *The 7 habits of highly effective people, powerful lessons in personal change,* New York, NY: Simon & Schuster, 10, 206-216.

Cranton, P. (1994). *Understanding and promoting transformative learning,* San Francisco, CA: Jossey-Bass, 28, 92-120.

Daley, B. (2001). *Learning and professional practice: A study of four professions,* Adult Education Quarterly, Adult Education Research Conference, November, 2001.

Dietze, E. V. (2001). *Paradigms explained: rethinking Thomas Kuhn's philosophy of science,* Westport, CT, Greenwood Publishing Group, Inc., 52, 23-75.

Doob, C. B. (1994). *Sociology: an introduction,* (4th ed.). Orlando FL, Harcourt Brace & Company, 338-339.

Driscoll, M. (2006) *Rich or poor, it's righteousness that really matters* http://seattletimes.nwsource.com/html/faithvalues/2003112927_driscoll08.html

Encarta (2009, March 18). *Encarta world English dictionary,* Retrieved from http://encarta.msn.com/dictionary_1861605083/discourage.html?partner=orp

Erikson, E. H. (1950). *Growth and crisis of the healthy personality.* In M.J.E. Senn  (Eds.). Symposium on the Healthy Personality. Supplement II. New York: Josiah Macy, Jr. Foundation, 55, 91-146.

Eraut, M. (2002). *Developing professional knowledge and competence,* Washington D.C., Falmer Press, 147, 5-152.

Gates, B. & Gate, M. Retrieved February 17, 2009. *Bill and Melinda Gates foundation,* http://www.gatesfoundation.org/grants/Pages/overview.aspx)

Graham, S. (1997). *You can make it happen,* New York, NY: Simon & Schuster, 60, 60-120.

Greenleaf, K. R. (1977). *Servant leadership: a journey into the nature of legitimate power and greatness,* Mahwah NJ, Robert K. Greenleaf Ctr. 162.

Haddad, S. (1996). *Adult education: the legislative and policy environment,* 1 International Review of Education, Vol 42, Nos, 2,1-3.

Hume, David (1777). *The empiricist; An enquiry concerning human understanding,* Fellow of University College, Oxford, Section II, 317.

Ke Akua, A., & Apollo, A., (2007). *3rd to 4th, 5th, 6th, and 7th dimensions explained* (http://people.tribe.net/adamapollo/blog/9141f47 a-1db2-44bb-8bb6-a28e09827153 Retrieved April 10, 2009.

Knapper, C. & Cropley, A. (2000). *Lifelong learning in higher education.* (3rd ed.), London: Kogan Page Limited, 45.

Kuhn, T. S. (1962). *The structure of scientific revolution* (2nd ed.), Chicago IL, The University of Chicago Press, 24.

Lindeman, C. E. (1966). *The meaning of adult education,* Norman, OK, New Republic, 19, 41-60.

Martin, W. A. (2004). 13th Annual African American & Latino/A American Adult Education Research Symposium, *Eradicating complacency in public policy affecting communities of color,* Chicago IL, Northern Illinois University Graduate School, College of Education, Department of Counseling, 6, 69-75.

Martin, W. A., Geraldine W., Jordan, F., & Brady, C. (2002). 11th Annual African American & Latino/A American Adult Education Research Symposium, *The role of continuing professional education in lifelong learning: The RRRR Model,* Chicago IL, Northern Illinois University Graduate School, College of Education, Department of Counseling, 9, 84-93.

Merriam, S. & Caffarella, R.S. (1999). *Learning in adulthood: A comprehensive guide.* San Francisco: Jossey-Bass Inc. 206.

Mohammad, A. (1996). *Statistics for business and economics* (6th ed.). St. Paul MN, West Publishing, 41, 45-86.

Moore, N. B. & Bruder, K. (1996). *Philosophy: The power of ideas* (3rd ed.). Mountain View, CA: Mayfield Publishing, 34.

Mott, V. & Daley B. (2000). *Charting a course for continuing professional education: Reframing Professional Practice* (Eds.). San Francisco, CA: Jossey-Bass Publishers, No. 86. 29.

Ormrod, J. E. (1995). *Educational psychology principles and applications,* Englewood Cliff NJ, Prentice-Hall, Inc. 98.

Pace, R.C. (1972). *Education and evangelism,* Los Angeles, CA: McGraw-Hill, 96-97.

Pais, A. (1982). *The science and the life of Albert Einstein.* New York, NY: Oxford University Press, 15, 142-157.

Peters, T.J., & Waterman Jr. R.H., (1982). *In search of excellence: Lessons from America's best-run companies,* New York, NY: Harper & Row, Publishers, 55.

Pratt, D. & Nesbit, T. (2000). *Discourses and cultures of teaching.* In Wilson, A. and Hayes (Eds) (2000). <u>Handbook of adult and continuing education</u> San Francisco, CA: Jossey-Bass. 121.

Project H.O.M.E., (2008). *Local philanthropist challenges Philadelphia community to get creative about fundraising,* Retrieved December 14, 2008, http://www.projecthome.org/news/?id=107

Raiskums, B. W. (2001). *Principles and principals: A dictionary of contemporary adult education terms and their users,* Anchorage, AK: PWR & Associates, 9, 55-64.

Rathus, S.A. (1993). *Psychology* (5th ed.). New York, NY: Harcourt Brace College Publishers, 2, 726-728.

Smaldino, S. E., Lowther, D.L., & Russell, J.D. (2008). *Instructional technology and media for learning,* Upper Saddle River, NJ: Pearson Education, Inc., 20, 6-26.

Smith, C. A., Cudaback, D., Goddard, H. W., & Myers-Walls, J. A. (1994). *National extension parent education model of critical parenting practices,* Manhattan, KS: Kansas Cooperative Extension Service, 21, 75-96.

Smith-Phelan, L., Grassi, M., Caputo, C., Berman, J., Sheorey, R., Hart, M., & Ventura, K. (1997). *Sound and light,* Upper Saddle River, NJ: Prentice Hall, 57-58.

Starcevich, M. M. (1998). *Coach, mentor: Is there a difference?* Retrieved March 30, 2009 http://www.coachingandmentoring.com/Articles/mentoring.html

Stuckenberg, J.H.W. (1888). *Introduction to the study of philosophy* http://books.google.com/books?id=8lpKvxNgv1IC&pg=PA200&lpg=PA200&dq=state+of+nature+%2Bstuckenberg&source=bl&ots=hAT filK7q4&sig=yLJx-pkb9ziqeLBTCjBB9zpGQvw&hl=en&ei=CS37Sf6uH6KwMeDEjLEE&sa=X&oi=book_result&ct=result&resnum=1#PPP1,M1, retrieved May 1, 2009. 99, 198-399

*Webster's third new international dictionary,* (1986). Springfield, MA: Merriam-Webster Inc.

*Webster's dictionary of the English language unabridged* deluxe edition, (1977). New York, NY: Publishers International Press.

# Additional Readings

Allen, R. (1986). *Creating wealth,* New York, NY: Simon & Schuster, Inc.

Einstein, A. (1989). *Letter to Michele Besso's family.* Ref. Bernstein, Jeremy, *A critic at large: Besso.* The New Yorker.

Feynman, Richard, P. (1965). *Quantum mechanics and path integrals.* McGraw Hill, New York.

Jakes, T.D. (1995). *Loose the man & let him go! So you call yourself a Man?* New York, NY: First Inspirational Press.

Kiyosaki, R. T. (1998). *Rich dad, poor dad,* New York, NY: Time Warner Book Group.

Osteen, J. (1995). *Your best life now: 7 steps to living at your full potential,* Wheaton, IL: Tyndale House Publishers, Inc.

Osteen, J. (2005). *Daily readings from your best life now: 90 devotions for living at your full potential,* New York, NY: Joel Osteen Publishing.

Shapiro, R. (2001). *The power of nice,* New York, NY: Wiley & Sons, Inc.